WEST
at
WAR

James Belsey & Helen Reid

REDCLIFFE
Bristol

First published in 1990 by Redcliffe Press Limited
49 Park Street, Bristol

© James Belsey and Helen Reid

ISBN 0 948265 64 7

Published to coincide with a four-part television
series made for HTV West by Domino Films.

Typeset by and printed by WBC Limited
Bristol and Maesteg

WEST AT WAR

CONTENTS

Acknowledgments

The authors would like to thank the following for their help in preparing this book: Martin Chainey for his advice and assistance in selecting work by the late Jim Facey and Dave Facey for allowing his father's photographs to be reproduced; Gerry Brooke, Librarian, Bristol United Press; Bristol United Press; Bristol Reference Library; Wessex Newspapers; Imperial War Museum and Mrs Renee Meenehan.

t is half a century since the West Country went to war. Now, at last, the real picture of those momentous years is becoming clear. The echoes of the myths and half-truths, propaganda and censorship become fainter all the time.

The true story of the War In The West is very different from the long-accepted official version. Only recently, with hindsight and a lifetime's experience, have the participants found a new perspective on the jumble of emotions and events that marked the years 1939-45.

World War II has been mythologised. It was a natural process which began with contemporary propaganda, stridently patriotic films and literature and a desperate need to look on the bright side. The image was set: shoulders to the wheel, grim determination in adversity, the chirpy Cockney sparrow, dusting off the debris of the latest blitz and shaking his fist in defiance at the departing enemy. We can take it!

The reality was far more heroic: underfed, poorly clothed, terrified and exhausted men, women and children who, at the worst times, came to the very threshold of defeatism but found that extra ounce of courage to pull themselves back from despair – and who did take it.

The West Country experienced and survived almost all the extremes that World War II had to offer with the exception of attack by V-weapons. Mercifully, the region lay beyond the range of the dreaded doodlebugs or the phantom-like V2s which fell unseen and unheard until their thunderous detonation. It was spared that ordeal. But it was spared no others. The West's major cities were blitzed, with Bristol and Plymouth suffering appalling damage. Large towns were bombed, both Bath and Weston-super-Mare among them. Even small, seemingly peaceful country towns like Painswick were struck by German bombers.

The fear of death raining down from the skies, of gigantic aerial armadas crewed by soulless automatons, had haunted the between-the-wars years. It was a science fiction nightmare of a dreadful world to come. But the reality of living through full-scale air raids on densely populated cities and of coping with their aftermath proved much, much worse than any writer of fiction could have imagined. It was an extended, terrifying, seemingly endless ordeal which stretched nerves and morale to breaking point.

If the blitzes and lesser air raids and the disruption and misery they caused were the worst of the war in the West, the comradeship, the mounting excitement as the great armies gathered before the Normandy invasion and the powerful sense of national unity and purpose were among the best.

No one book can hope to tell the full story. Instead we have chosen to tell the tale through the voices of people who lived through those terrible, drab, exciting years. For some it was a stimulating, challenging time, when war work took them out of a dull, undemanding existence and expanded their horizons.

For some it was a time of numbing tragedy with family and friends killed, homes wrecked and lives scarred forever. For some who were children of the war, it was a time of novelty and excitement with everyday routine disrupted.

Now, half a century later, the combatants, the volunteers, the civilians and those who were children can look back on their experiences with the candour and honesty that comes from age, and matters that were once spoken in whispers can be admitted: the booing of war leader Winston Churchill on a tour of blitzed Bristol, the tinkering with newsreel film to give a false impression of morale, the secret reports which spoke of growing alarm at the worsening spirit of the people.

When some began to suggest this darker truth in histories written 20 or so years after the war, there was dismay, even outrage, as if the West Country's courage had been called into question. But the evidence had always been there, locked away in reports by Mass Observation.

Mass Observation, an independent grass roots social survey organisation, had been set up two years before the war began. Its purpose was to record the feelings and reactions of ordinary people and to report on selected topics. Its role in wartime has proved invaluable to later observers, offering a remarkable insight into the mood of the times. Its observers were anonymous and discreet. They would record the number of people carrying gas-masks, the number visiting pubs or cinemas, casual conversations in shops and places of entertainment which revealed the true state of morale.

Secret reports were also kept by police, local authorities and the Ministry of Information, but all too often their findings were unpalatable even a generation later. Half a century later the interviewees in this book which accompanies the series *The West At War* made by Domino Films for HTV confirm the truth: that there was great heroism and stoicism and cheerful camaraderie – and that there was also protest, panic and defeatism, bureaucratic bungling and disorganisation.

World War II has become part of not-so-recent history. Those too young to remember the times must strive hard to imagine what it must have been like and there are fewer and fewer physical reminders to stir the imagination. Soon there will be little left but the sawn-off stumps of roadside railings, cut down to be melted for munitions in the first, eager flush of activity at the start of the war and the occasional infill of a newer house standing incongruously in a period terrace or street, marking where a bomb fell and a house vanished in a deafening instant.

In the cities, the huge craters have long since been filled in. The ravaged shops, offices and factories cleared. The broken homes flattened. The ruined churches demolished, restored or, in a few, poignant instances, allowed to stand as chastening memorials to the death, destruction and suffering they witnessed in air raids and the blazing chaos which followed.

In the countryside, the old airfields are almost all returned to pasture or plough and the great military camps which once housed the huge, multi-national army which left to win back Europe have been swept away so thoroughly that returning veterans, trying to locate 'their' wartime station, can sometimes be found wandering, puzzled, in rural Avon, Gloucestershire, Somerset and Wiltshire, unable to recognise once-familiar surroundings. The lucky ones find locals who remember those days and who can direct them to where their canteens and huts, parade grounds and mess halls once stood.

But if time has blurred and even effaced the vestiges of that war, the memories linger and, with retrospect, become more distinct. Their story is a moving part of our social history.

1. In the front line

Behind the statistics of the war in the West Country lie hundreds of personal tragedies. Gladys Locke, just 19 when war broke out, was to be a casualty of the very first air raid to hit Bristol, on the night of June 24/25.

‘On June 23, 1940, against my mother's wishes, I got married in Brislington at a ceremony that was really a comedy. My mother and my husband's mother nearly had a punch up, and the vicar asked us if we wanted to change our minds! We went to Weston-super-Mare for the honeymoon, and the next morning, my husband was nowhere to be seen. Then he came in with a face as long as a fiddle and said 'France has capitulated.' I didn't even know what the word meant. But I had a terrible feeling, an awful feeling which I sometimes get now, I've got to get home, whatever happens. So we got the train back to Bristol, and everyone was amazed to see us. Eventually we got to bed, and I was standing there in my nightgown, when the siren went. We'd heard it before in practices, and we didn't take much notice, but this time I said 'let's go down to the shelter.'
My mother said 'don't be silly, it's only a practice' but I said 'Oh no it isn't, I know something's going to happen tonight.' Anyway we did go down to the shelter, a matter of yards, and the bombs were already dropping, and I was shaking and screaming. First came the incendiary bombs, you could tell because the whole garden was lit up, and then came a bomb. The force of the blast took the top of the shelter off, it was like Armageddon. I thought it was the end. All the windows of our house were gone, the doors were off, there was water rushing out because the pipes had been hit, the roof was off, and part of the wall. Nearly everything that was breakable in the house was broken, even the linen in the drawers was ripped. All my wedding presents were gone, even my wedding cake, which was full of glass. We had to throw it away. I was absolutely terrified, scared stiff, because you see we hadn't had any experience of anything like that before.’

Gladys Locke developed a hysterical fear of the raids, which later was made worse by the horrifying experience she had in the November raids on Bristol. So Gladys, now pregnant, became one of Bristol's 'trekkers', the people who left the city nightly for the safety of the countryside. In the bitter autumn and winter of 1940, she, her husband and her arthritic mother would set out with a blanket and a thermos, for the unknown, sleeping in ditches and lanes and huts – anything was preferable to facing the rain of bombs on the city.

Previous page: A new sight in the city at night, as anti-aircraft tracer and searchlights carve up the night sky.

‘We didn't leave Bristol every night, just nights when I had a feeling there would be a raid. . . I'd say 'let's go to Keynsham, or Long Ashton.' I just had an instinct where to go, and followed my nose. My husband just came to humour me because I got so scared. We would walk miles and sleep in a field, or doze rather, or go to a shelter in a village, and stay there till the early hours of the morning when there was a bus to get us home. You'd never believe the places we slept in, so cold and damp. I never cared what it was like, so long as we were out of the raids. You could see the city burning and I would think 'thank God we're not in it'. After a few weeks of this I was in such a state that we took lodgings in Compton Dando. I didn't tell the woman I was pregnant.

Then one night in late December I went into labour. I didn't realise it, I thought it was indigestion, and the doctor was called. He picked me up and wrapped me in a blanket and took me to Keynsham Workhouse, because there was a raid on in Bristol, and it was the only place he could take me. The last thing I remember was saying 'am I going to die?' and then they gave me morphia, and I didn't know a thing about the birth at all. When I came to, I was still lying on the labour bed, and they said unfortunately the baby had died because it was premature. But I heard it crying, heard it whimpering, it wasn't dead. And they gave it to me, and it was a perfectly beautiful baby. Of course I was drugged to the eyeballs, and I fell asleep, holding the baby. Oh I was happy, ever so happy.

The next morning I asked for my baby and the matron said 'now you get better and be a good girl and you shall have your baby.' But it had died in the night. My husband knew it, but I didn't. So I had my baby christened, Michael John, and he was buried, and I spent Christmas in hospital, I was there for several weeks. And when I came out, I just couldn't bear to look at a baby, if I saw a pram I'd walk miles to get away. When my sister had her baby, I just couldn't bear to stay in the house. I'm sure it happened because of the trekking, of course it did, all that fear, and walking miles and sleeping out in the cold . . . I had no medical attention. If I'd looked after myself, the baby would have been all right. But my fear of the raids was so great. After that, for a while, I didn't want to live any more. I wanted to die, like my baby. **,**

No-one could have imagined or predicted a tragedy like this, in the last months of peace during 1939.

When the lights went out all over the West Country on September 3, it was goodbye to a different world. The West was still smarting from the long haul of the Depression years, of the dole queues and the hated Means Test, and in the rural areas, farming was still virtually unmechanised and life was hard. It was still a world full of rigid social barriers, but one which was beginning to improve for the working class. The worst of the Bristol slums had been cleared and 65,000 occupants moved to the nine new council estates which ringed the city.

But the poor were still suffering from malnutrition: a Bristol University survey in 1938 found that some 40,000 Bristol families were living in poverty in the city, at a time when it was estimated that a family of man, wife and three children needed 37s. 6d. a week, excluding rent money, to live on. They found that a fifth of the working class families were unable to give their children a proper start in life, and tests had proved that children in Bristol state schools were inches shorter and pounds lighter then their counterparts in the private and public schools.

As citizens all over the West carefully put up their blackout that first night, they were facing the unknown. But in a way, the announcement of war on that sunny Sunday brought relief as well as resignation. The possibility of war had been hanging over their heads for a long time and now the waiting was over. But the mood was sombre.

For what kind of war was it going to be? There had been reminders of how weapons technology and aerial warfare had advanced in the bloody battles of

JF

An evocative photograph of an ARP warden at the ready in a Bristol suburb.

the Spanish Civil War. No bombs had ever fallen on the West Country during World War I, but this time round, they knew it would be different and deadly, with the war being fought on home territory. They were going to be in the front line, and it was a frightening prospect.

Tess Broughton was a young mother at the outbreak of war.

‘Having lost both my parents in the first war, I imagined we were all going to be killed immediately, and that the Germans would invade straight away.’

So did Irene Crew.

‘The day war was declared we were all stunned and very agitated. We were saying to one another where are we going to hide?’

For the children, war was something exciting and rather novel. Gerald Smith was a young schoolboy at the time.

‘We were at chapel near home, and it was a gorgeous sunny morning. This fellow walked in and went up to the minister and said that war had been declared and would we quietly leave the chapel and go to our houses and listen to the radio. That seemed to be the important thing, to listen to the radio. Parents

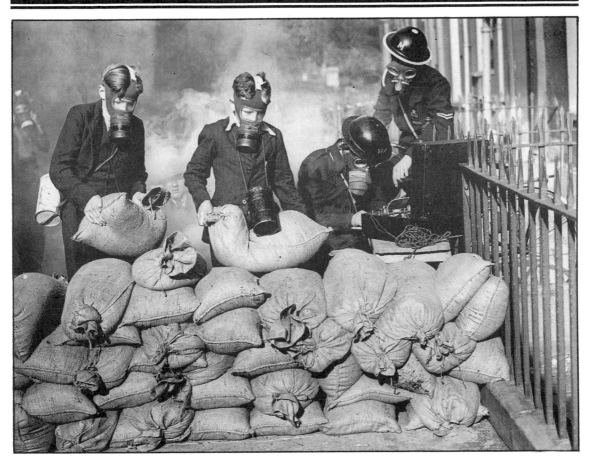

were frightened, the grown-ups were frightened, but it was exciting for us, because of the troops about and the soldiers with guns. We realised from that moment our lives were going to change. At first we thought we would be attacked that very night but later they assured us that aeroplanes would never reach Bristol and that the war would last perhaps 12 months. **'**

Civil Defence rehearsal during the phoney war.

And overnight, things did change. For a start all the theatres and cinemas closed for a fortnight, so that people did not even have entertainment to take war off their minds. All they could do was listen to the radio which in the first days seemed to provide nothing but endless music from Sandy McPherson at the organ, interspersed with news bulletins and instructions.

' The anxiety and fear built up, we sensed it in our parents and it overflowed to the children. People seemed to be rushing abut everywhere and doing things that you hadn't noticed before, going down to the shops and stocking up with food – they even did it on the Sunday war was declared, when the shops weren't open anyway. They seemed to think it was all going to happen at once. **'**

It was just as well that things did not all happen at once, for the cities and towns of the West, like elsewhere, were not entirely ready for war. The newspapers were full of appeals for more firemen, more ARP volunteers, more

Gas mask drill, September 1939.

first aiders, more equipment. Gas-masks were yet to be distributed to everyone, and the major fear was that the Germans would use gas straight away. Memories of the gassed troops of World War One were still vivid.

Gerald Smith remembers a chaotic mock gas attack:

'One day we heard there was going to be a test in our area. Gas was going to be released and at the sound of a siren, everyone had to put on gas masks, because they were going to throw gas canisters. After a few minutes with the gas masks on, the children thought it would be rather funny to smell the gas, to see what happened, so they took off their masks, and the grown-ups thought the test was over and took off theirs as well. Everybody started to cry, the tears ran from their eyes, the whole thing was a flop, it was a complete fiasco. And then one of the gas canisters exploded and everyone ran away.'

Nor were there enough shelters: the Home Office had estimated that Bristol needed 25,000 places in public shelters and when war broke out there were just 3,500 ready. Moreover these brick surface shelters were built, it turned out, with the wrong formula for the mortar; had they been hit, they would have crumpled like a deck of cards and the concrete roofs would have crushed the inhabitants. Bristol needed 2,000 ambulances but only 50 were available, and the fire service was desperately short of men and equipment. Second-hand cars and lorries were bought, and they promptly broke down.

Then there was the hated blackout to deal with. It was enforced that Sunday night, after a few all too light-hearted rehearsals in the last months of peace, and caused many civilian accidents, long before the real war began. In Bristol, 78 people survived falling into the floating harbour; cars, having to drive along

pitch dark roads on masked sidelights only, crashed into one another and into trees, or into pedestrians stumbling along with only the light of a torch whose bulb was muffled with tissue paper. For city-dwellers, it was if their town had suddenly been moved into the depths of the country. RAF planes were asked to fly over Bristol to see if the blackout was effective, and reported that the city was indeed dark, but easily recognisable because the moonlight glinted on the waterways in the city – and no-one could think how to camouflage water.

A new sight for children: men marching in gas masks, on The Downs, 1939.

Gradually there were slight improvements; white lines were painted down the centre of roads and proved such a boon that they became a permanent feature; kerbstones were painted white and trees had white rings painted round their trunks. Motorists painted their mudguards and runningboards white, and people took to wearing light coloured clothing at night to make themselves visible to traffic. Firms selling blackout materials, sandbags and shelters did a roaring trade.

The preparations for war had been going on since 1938, with the first Anderson shelters, free to those with an income under £250 a year, and £6 to £7 for the rest. They began to arrive by the thousand, but gas masks, first issued in September 1938, ran short in Bristol and huge crowds built up outside the Colston Hall, where they were to be fitted and issued. Joyce Storey went to collect hers.

❝When the first delivery did arrive, people behaved in a most uncivilised way, they pushed and shoved and fought for those dreadful things, because we were sure that poison gas would be used on us . . . when you went out it became a kind of ritual to say 'don't forget gas mask, identity card, torch.'❞

Within the photograph:
F.26 BOOKED UP WARDENS POST.

EARPLUGS
THESE ARE BEING ISSUED
HERE TODAY IDENTITY
CARDS MUST BE SHOWN
SEE LIST OF ROADS
IN THIS POST AREA.
ADULTS MUST APPLY

An Air Raid Warden hands out ear plugs in preparation for the blitz.

For the first fortnight of the war all was strange and busy and threatening, and then normality of a kind returned. All the places of entertainment opened up again, so that you could see Leslie Howard and Wendy Hiller in *Pygmalion*, or Robert Donat in *Goodbye Mr. Chips*, catch a musical at the Princes Theatre or go to a carefully blacked-out pub. The middle classes continued to advertise, mostly in vain, for servants and people settled down to get on with the Phoney War. There were irritating shortages of things like torch batteries, and runs on tea and coffee as rumours spread that supplies were running out.

Bristol's Lady Mayoress announced that she would not be At Home "owing to the international situation", at Weston-super-Mare folk still sat in the September sunshine and posters went up everywhere telling citizens to do this and not to do that. Wally Hammond came top of the batting averages, followed by Len Hutton and Denis Compton, and Bristol City drew their first match of the season . . . life seemed to be going on much as usual. The *Evening Post* told citizens of good old mercantile Bristol "let buying and selling go on", fearing the spectre of unemployment.

Meanwhile the Civil Defence of the region was getting into shape. A Regional Commissioner, Sir Hugh Elles, was appointed to be in charge of the South West, which he administered from an office in Bristol. Under him, each local authority had to run a complex system of services: social and welfare teams to care for the housing and feeding of the homeless, casualty services to deal with medical care, engineering teams for rescue and house repair and demolition, the fire service, the ARP, and communications.

Each of these services was run by a committee and a member from each of them made up an Emergency Committee which dealt with day to day crises. As well as this official civil defence network, there were military authorities for

each district, and scores of voluntary organisations whose work would have to mesh in. It was a bureaucratic nightmare, and it is little wonder that communications were garbled and muddles arose. Often it was not clear who was supposed to do what.

For the rural areas, the immediate problem was to deal with the flood of evacuees who were arriving in the so-called safe West Country. From September 1 the great exodus from London began, and weary, grubby children dressed in cast-offs descended on the astonished but willing countryfolk. Some of the evacuees from the East End had never slept in a bed or eaten at a table before, and for the middle class and rural hosts, their arrival was an eye-opener to the poverty that still existed in Britain.

The country had been divided into at risk, neutral and reception areas, and most of the West Country came into this last category, an astonishing decision when viewed with hindsight. It seems amazing that the War Office should have thought that Bristol, a major port and a shipbuilding city, home to dozens of major engineering firms and to Bristol Aeroplane Company, the biggest aircraft and engine manufacturer in the country, would be strategically unimportant to the Germans.

Nor did they foresee that with the fall of France, Avonmouth would be vital as the one of the few ports which faced out to the free world, when the need for supplies and troops was crucial. So no Bristol children were evacuated, unless their parents arranged a billet privately, and paid over the official rate, 10s. 6d.

A Home Guard exercise, checking an identity card at a road block on the Downs, 1940.

"Unaccompanied
children" had to wear
luggage labels to help
speed them on their
way to their
evacuation billets.
This pair is checked
at Temple Meads.

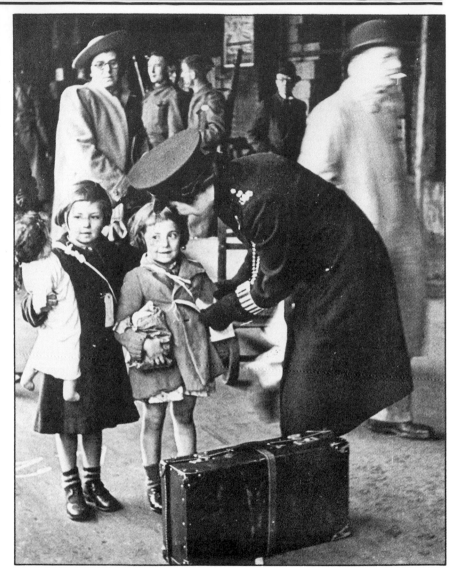

for the first child, and 8s. 6d. for subsequent ones. All the places that Bristol
children might have gone to nearby were filled up with Londoners, a fact that
was to cause problems later on.

And Somerset turned out to be an essential area for air bases and later for the
American troops preparing for D-day – yet it was Somerset that bore the brunt
of the evacuation plans. By August 1940, there were 24,776 unaccompanied
children – and with helpers, mothers and extra teachers, the total came to
27,527 people to be billeted. By January 1941, this figure had increased to
62,874, and this was apart from the 56,682 war workers who had come into the
county. The wartime population of Somerset virtually doubled and the county
was bursting at the seams. Whole schools moved west, and stately homes like
Longleat and Lacock Abbey became homes for school children.

That first wave of evacuees in September 1939, was the tangible evidence of war, and local billetting officers, teachers, clergy, WVS and WI members did marvels organising places for these bewildered and homesick children, whose new homes ranged to anything from a farm labourer's cottage to a local mansion. Lifestyles clashed as the streetwise London children came up against their rural counterparts, and suddenly class sizes doubled at schools never built to cope with such numbers. There was a slight easing of the overcrowding when some of the evacuees left during the phoney war, but a second wave, whose story is related in Chapter Two, came back when the London and provincial blitzes began. And ironically Somerset did not turn out to be the entirely safe haven it was supposed to be, as bombs began to fall in 1940, with raids on Banwell, Taunton, Yeovil and Bridgwater, all 'safe' areas.

Gloucestershire was another refuge for city children. Audrey Sparks came from London's Docklands to live in the Wye valley with an elderly couple, in 1939, and loved the experience.

❮I fell in love with their lovely house. I'd never seen anything but a Docklands council flat shaped like a rectangular box and their house was all curves and niches and rounded bays. My foster-parents had masses of books, too, and I'd literally never seen one. What did it matter to me that they were old when they were so kind?❯

Barry Saloman at the age of seven went from East Ham to a big house with a swimming pool and an orchard, in Wiltshire.

❮I'd come from a two up, two down house with no bathroom. My host was a major in the artillery and his house was out of this world. They had a maid and I'd never seen such an abundance of food.❯

A rather different set of evacuees were the staff of the BBC. The Light Entertainment, Variety, Drama, Music and Religious Affairs departments were sent to Bristol in 1939, and the Whiteladies Road establishment jumped from 70 people to 900. Various church halls in Clifton were adapted to become recording studios.

The extra staff found homes in the city – the standard charge was a guinea a week – and Bristolians had to get used to exotic, bohemian bearded figures with a taste for Bristol's sherry.

Amongst the famous that came were Jack Warner, star of Garrison Theatre, Arthur Askey and Richard 'Stinker' Murdoch with *Bandwaggon*, Henry Hall and of course Tommy Handley, star of ITMA.

The producer of ITMA, Francis Worsley recalls:

❮On September 19, 1939, at 9.30 pm, ITMA had its first night. After a two-hour rehearsal, a long time for those early days of the war, we took the floor in Clifton Parish Hall before a small audience mainly composed of people on the staff. We had to be very strict about the tiniest glimmer of light, because of the blackout, and we had to creep into various studios around a complicated system of screens and curtains, carrying our gasmasks wherever we went. But once inside the building all was gaiety and light, and a sort of party spirit pervaded the atmosphere. There was no stage, so that the audience and the artists were all together on the same level, and when they were not actually performing the cast sat down, often on the grand piano or on the floor, giving the whole thing a very informal air. Thus it was that the first night of the show that was destined to

Cheerful propaganda
picture of happy
Bristol evacuees
leaving by train from
Temple Meads.

make radio history. Tommy's first words set the topical pace at which we tried
to keep going ever since: 'Hello folks! it's Mein Kampf again, Sorry, I should
say Hello folks! It's that MAN again. That was a Goebbled version. . .'

ITMA became a national institution and its characters, Colonel Chinstrap,
Mrs. Mop ('can I do you now sir?'), Cecil and Claude, and Poppy Pooh-Pah
became national heroes. But Tommy Handley himself was not happy in Bristol.
He was homesick and developed the habit of going to Bristol Zoo to stare mourn-
fully at the monkeys and particularly at Alfred, the caged gorilla with whom he
seemed to share a special sympathy.

Garrison Theatre was also broadcast from Clifton Parish Hall, and its star
Jack Warner came to Bristol to offer his services. The show was supposed to be
performed by men from the services in front of the troops, and Warner, out of
work at the time, was judged perfect for the cheeky cockney soldier. He

invented the expression 'blue pencil' to signify the deletion of a swear word and this became a national catchphrase, as did 'Mind My Bike'. Warner remembers:

> ❝Every week we used to try to work out a different way for me to come in. One time I'd come in from the wings, another I'd come up through the orchestra, and one week I decided I'd ride through the stalls on a bike, shouting 'Mind My Bike' as I came.❞

The BBC Symphony Orchestra also moved to Bristol with their conductor Sir Adrian Boult, who became a familiar figure shopping in Whiteladies Road, and conducting his musicians in the Colston Hall. The BBC studios in Bristol became a paradise for young autograph hunters.

But once again, Bristol was not to prove a safe haven. The studios themselves came under attack, and during one raid, The Epilogue went out with announcer Stuart Hibbert reading while lying on the floor under the table, while violinist Paul Beard tried to play Bach's *Air on a G String* on his knees. In 1941, the BBC's evacuees left Bristol for safer venues.

People were not the only ones to be sent west: national treasures ended up in new homes all over the region. Bristol Corporation spent £8,000 bomb-proofing a tunnel by the Portway for the storage of its city archives and regalia. The Victoria and Albert Museum sent some of its finest pieces to Montacute House, where they were kept under guard, and the British Museum sent 500 boxes of precious manuscripts to be stored in an air-conditioned underground quarry at Westwood near Corsham.

Avening in Gloucestershire and Northwick Park near Bristol were other hosts to art treasures, and Somerset churches took in ecclesiastic masterpieces, ranging from sets of bells, pews, fonts, and plate to whole organ cases. The strangest evacuee of all was the priceless Domesday Book, which secretly spent the war – along with other valuable early manuscripts from the Public Record Office – in a disused prison in Shepton Mallet.

Another kind of transfer to the countryside was going on, as the first calls for women workers came and the city girls opted for a healthier life on the land. The Land Army, formed in the First World War, was re-established in 1939, for 50,000 jobs of farm labourers who had gone to war had to be filled. The girls were given a month's training before being sent to a farm where they earned sevenpence halfpenny an hour and often worked from dawn to dusk as well as doing household chores.

Mabs Holland went to a farm on the Badminton Estate, where she says, she was a disaster.

> ❝I couldn't milk, I fell over the cows in the dark and though I didn't actually crash a tractor, I did knock a silo down. . . I thought it would be rather nice to drive a tractor rather than a horse and cart. So John, the farmer's son whom I subsequently married long after, showed me how to drive it and he said now keep going straight. So I did and I hit the silo. After that I went to a beautiful farm at Bradford-on-Avon where they had about 125 pedigree Guernseys, and they had to be groomed like you would race-horses, their tails had to be washed and combed. These cows had piped music in their stalls, it was amazing.❞

But in the early days, many Land Army girls felt they were being exploited. Mabs Holland:

Women go into
uniform: a recruiting
station for the
Women's Auxiliary
Territorial Service.

‘Nobody minds doing her share in the house she's living in, but the majority of farmers expected you to do a great deal of the domestic work, which was not what you were there for: it rather took the edge off your patriotism after a 12 or 14 hour day. We were exploited as cheap labour.’

Claire Wallis found herself working for the Duchess of Beaufort at Badminton.

‘The royals would roll up their sleeves and help. Queen Mary sawed logs, Princess Alexandra used to help me clean out the goats. The farm was the Duchess's hobby. She had great big cows with names like Badminton Diana, and it was my job to bring them in at night. Because they were black and you couldn't use your torch on account of the blackout, you couldn't see them unless you actually tripped over them. Invariably when I eventually arrived back, the Duchess would say to me in her high-pitched voice 'You're late! You're sacked!' Of course she re-instated me the next day.’

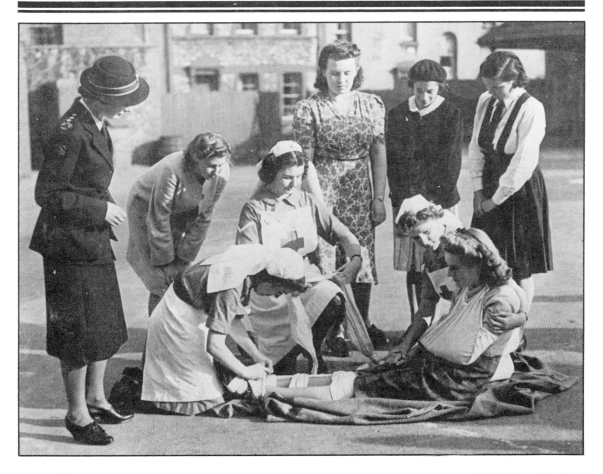

Phyllis Wyatt went to various farms in Somerset:

❛I went first to a small general one where I didn't learn much but spent a lot of time milking, while the boss and his workman sat in the cider house, tippling. Then I went to a smaller farm where I did everything: I cut thistles and hedges, chain-harrowed with shire horses, worked with sheep, planted and hoed, harvested the root crops, cut kale, picked apples and made corn ricks . . . it was farming in the old-fashioned style, no tractors and lots of hard work, but I enjoyed every minute of it and look back to those days as some of the happiest of my life.❜

A Red Cross Youth group training at Fairfield Grammar School, Bristol. As trained women were called up to do war work, more young first aiders were urgently needed.

Other women volunteered to work in the new Auxiliary Fire Service, amongst them Mary Palmer of Henleaze, Bristol.

❛I had to find part of the uniform and clothes were on coupons so my shirt was an old one of my father's and the tie was one of his funeral ties. I had no black shoes so I dyed a pair of old light ones. I felt very smart. We trained as firefighters for two weeks but I was landed with women's work, because the men were in charge. I had the job of making snacks for the men on duty. Our first job was to cook them sprats: we coped as best we could but were mortified afterwards when one of them said 'we thought you would have gutted and

JF

Soldiers investigate a German bomber plane shot down near Long Ashton.

filleted them first.' From November 1940 on, I found myself called to the station several times a night. When on alert we would mainly make cups of tea and chat. It was a hazardous journey reporting for duty with ack-ack shrapnel falling all around. Many a time we had to lie down in the street and on one occasion a large piece of shrapnel hit me on my tin hat. The firemen loved to see us arrive, not because we did anything special but I think they got a morale-boost because we used to laugh and chat and it eased the tension.'

And so 1939 turned into 1940, rationing came, and the West learned to live with the Phoney War, the air raid rehearsals, the blackout, and the evacuees. Social life flourished and the pubs were full, despite the ever-weakening beer. Bristolians still waited for a further 800 Anderson shelters to arrive, and shelter building was held up by a lack of bricks.

Spring 1940 was breath-takingly beautiful and city people poured out to the still tranquil countryside, at the weekends. A false sense of security began to pervade the atmosphere: perhaps the West really was out of the enemy's reach. The bubble really burst when France fell in June.

Some sense of urgency had arrived with the formation that May of the Local Defence Volunteers, the LDV, or Look, Duck and Vanish, later to become the Home Guard, affectionately known then and now as Dad's Army. Bill Graves, then a teenager in Bristol, joined the LDV.

'I joined because I was bored with the ARP. We were given some khaki clothes which didn't fit and they gave us walking sticks and shot guns that they had borrowed – one chap had a fowling piece that dated from 1725. Gradually we got a few rifles and then we got serge uniforms and were trained by men who

JF

The horror of war: the remains of a German pilot, shot down at Stapleton, had to be scooped up in a wheelbarrow.

had learned drill in the Boer War. Yet we had this feeling, if Hitler comes, we're going to be OK. We were very short of ammunition, you used to get five rounds given to you and when the next guy came along, you handed them on to him. We also had bayonets and pikes which wouldn't fit the rifles. We went on exercises to practise for the invasion, with a Lewis gun that had no magazine and if the Germans had dropped on us, we wouldn't have stood a cat's chance in hell; I mean we would have gone down fighting, or run like hell. It was an absolute farce: on one occasion they put us up against the Irish Guards in a training exercise and they nearly killed us.

The news reels were always showing the Home Guard shooting down planes and so on but this is what really happened . . . we were cleaning weapons one afternoon when a low flying aircraft came over, so we nipped onto the roof of a building, filled a belt, loaded it and fired off a burst. We thought we were going to get a medal or something, but instead we got a rocket. I was told by the Captain that we had fired 27 rounds and that these rounds were threepence each, 'you can't just go shooting at aeroplanes like that', he said. It was crazy.'

The Dad's Army image was perilously near the truth. Norman Allan, who was a messenger in the ARP at first, also joined the LDV.

'My father knew a man who'd been in the Spanish Civil War, and he had his own ideas on the way in which we should defend ourselves, so he arranged for me to go on a course to learn guerilla fighting. I came back to my squad and started to tell them the way we ought to fight, with molotov cocktails and so on. An officer came forward and said 'stop all this, it is most ungentlemanly'. A lot of the officers were ex-servicemen from the last war and even the Boer War and they were very outdated in their approach. It wasn't until the fear of invasion was past that we got any sophisticated weapons at all. **9**

For all that, the Home Guard in Somerset, under-equipped as they were, actually did come face to face with the enemy: 27 German planes were to crash or be shot down in the county and 72 of their crew were captured, mostly by Dad's Army men, often unarmed.

The activities of the teenagers and dads of the Home Guard and the increasing anti-invasion activity began to make the West look more war-like. Concrete anti-tank traps appeared on the roads, barbed wire on the beaches, and thousands of pill-boxes, some cunningly disguised, were built. Camouflage dodges arrived; the cars at BAC's Filton car park were covered in camouflage netting and the roof of the Westland aircraft factory at Yeovil was disguised to look like a field from the air.

It all made sense when France fell on June 24: suddenly invasion became a real possibility. Early that month the Ministry of Health told the Bristol and Gloucester civil authorities to be ready for the reception of 'certain refugees'. They turned out to be the battle-weary dazed men who had been rescued from Dunkirk, in a defeat which the British managed to turn into a victory.

The soldiers limped into Bristol from the trains which arrived at Stapleton Road and Temple Meads, and filled every barracks space available, until someone had a brainwave and suggested using the temporary buildings put up in Eastville Park for a municipal exhibition which had been cancelled because of the outbreak of war.

Bristolians heard on the grapevine that the soldiers had arrived and went to shake hands with these tattered heroes. They went to the shops and bought all the snacks and sweets and cigarettes they could find to give to the men and 880 pies, the entire stock of a Bristol manufacturer, were bought up, and distributed. Clothes were donated, and private householders offered the filthy oil-stained men the use of their bathrooms. They left baths stained with oil and bath-mats covered in sand, and Bristolians like Bill Henton had to scour the shops for more soap.

6 We had as many as nine soldiers queueing to have a bath. Two of the men stayed long enough to become friends and they wrote a little poem of thanks. It went:

> From Dunkirk to Bristol with Jerry overhead,
> We are happy and cheerful though we should be dead.
> We've met with hospitality and tons of cigarettes.
> And we thank you all most heartily,
> Two lads of the BEF. **9**

The suffering of the soldiers at Dunkirk really brought home the reality of war, and later Bristolians learned that four of its much loved paddle-steamers had done their part in the rescue. The 'Brighton Belle' and the 'Brighton Queen', the 'Devonia' and 'The Glendower' had acted as shields while the

The weary and filthy Dunkirk survivors being kitted out at a Bristol depot.

men were taken off into the small ships, and two of them sank during the action.

Now Britain stood alone, and preparations against invasion began in earnest. Reports coming in from France and the other occupied countries fuelled the invasion scare and imagination ran riot. It was a frightening time, says Gerald Smith.

❝ We knew what Hitler was like and we thought what our lives would be like under dictatorship. ❞

The great fear was of German paratroopers dropping from the skies, and the Home Guard became ever more vigilant, according to Babs Atherton, who was in the ARP at Weston-super-Mare.

‘Weston's defence against invasion was one man at the far end of the pier, out to sea, with a torch, one halfway down the pier with a wooden stave or club and one at the entrance with a rifle and a telephone to alert headquarters if the invasion started.’

Comical false alarms often happened: Isabell Shaddick remembers an incident in Brislington, Bristol.

‘There was this chap, he was in the ARP, but he was in ordinary clothes that day. Some bells started ringing so he immediately announced 'Oh my God, we're being invaded, I shall have to change into my uniform.' Bells were only supposed to be rung if the enemy arrived.’

In Somerset, recalls Jack Symes, there was a full scale alert of the Home Guard, the only one of the war.

‘I was in the Home Guard in Somerset and we were called out in the middle of the night because of a report that paratroopers were coming down, and in some of the villages the church bells were rung, even though it was prohibited. It turned out that because it was a windy night, the haycocks in the fields were blowing up in the air and going across the field and coming down again, and in the moonlight they looked like parachutes landing, so one zealous Dad's Army man had sounded the alarm.’

In July there were reports that 14 parachutists had landed at Stinchcombe in Gloucestershire, and an extensive search was made, with no results.

Spy mania was one product of the invasion scare. The Home Guard held absurd exercises where they had to detect one of their number, disguised as a woman, as 'she' biked around the countryside doing suspicious things.

Bill Graves heard Home Guard lectures on how to spot a spy.

‘We were told that if strangers started asking you questions, we had to find out who they were and if they had foreign accents, and to challenge them to say 'Wendle Wilkie'. Apparently a German would have said 'Vendle Vilkie' and then you would have him, and bring him in. There were actually posters up in the Home Guard Headquarters showing you how to recognise the Fifth Column: most of them wore long black coats and black hats and had Hitler moustaches, and drove a big car. If I'd met one of them I would have run like the devil.’

Fifth columnists were suspected everywhere, and anyone who voiced any criticism of the way the war was being run was immediately suspected of being a Communist or a subversive. There was disorder at Filwood Park, Bristol when police investigated the issue of 'subversive' pamphlets and the editor of the Bristol Co-op publication *The Citizen* had his house searched because someone had informed on him.

Iris Caple's family came under suspicion, during the early raids on Bristol.

‘I was in our bungalow on my own when an army officer came to the door, very officious, and said he wanted to know if we had any mirrors in the house. He looked around and then explained that every time the ack-ack guns fired on the hill, someone was flashing a mirror. When my brother came home and I told him, he said bloody hell, and took me out into the garden. He'd propped bits of broken mirror all around, to catch the sun and help the plants grow, and these were flashing every time the guns fired!**'**

Gladys Locke remembers the case of the Bristol Mother Superior who was arrested as a spy.

'On the site of the HTV studios at Arno's Court there was the Convent of the Good Shepherd, a sort of children's home run by nuns. The Mother Superior was an Italian and she used to signal to the aeroplanes with a torch or a lamp, we thought it was Morse Code. The local people were up in arms about it and eventually she was taken away and interned. Probably she wasn't doing anything at all, but if she hadn't been taken away I'm sure the local people would have hanged her from the nearest tree.**'**

Civilians were forbidden to use cameras and it was this which made Mrs. Irene Towler suspicious when she saw a man photographing the railway line and gasometers at Barton Hill, Bristol.

'He came down our street every day at 11 am, and I saw he had a camera in his pocket. This went on for a few weeks all round Barton Hill and I informed the police, and they said they would come the next day. I was to follow him and I watched him go to Days Bridge where he was caught red-handed by the police. He was found to have a lot of incriminating stuff in his pockets, including a gun and a map of Bristol.**'**

While civilians were worrying about the invasion, the authorities were making secret plans to cope if it actually happened.

The entire South-West region would have been run from cellars under nos. 19 and 20 Woodland Road, in Clifton, Bristol. Here was the War Room, bomb-proofed with heavy metal doors and steel girders, where Sir Hugh Elles, the Regional Commissioner would have organised survival and resistance under a Nazi regime.

He would have kept in touch with five counties through a secret communications network and information would have been sent out to local administrators via a fleet of local schoolgirl and schoolboy messengers who could have gone about their normal life undetected, it was thought. The BBC, removed to a tunnel on the Portway, would have kept the public informed.

All the anti-invasion plans were kept in a War Book of which only three copies were ever made: if there was a chance that they should fall into enemy hands, they were to be destroyed. The plans were amazingly detailed. They explained how prisoners in West jails should be dispersed, they listed the locality of local wells and springs, the number of privately owned tractors and handcarts, and contained complete lists of local people who could keep essential services going. Printers had been lined up to print leaflets telling the public how to treat the enemy, and details were recorded about secret food stores – and how to destroy them if it looked as if they were going to fall into enemy hands – and there was even a detailed scheme for bread rationing.

Not surprisingly, there were also grim instructions on how to prepare mass graves. For the great fear was that an invasion would cause a panicky unplanned exodus into the countryside, with thousands of refugees clogging the roads, and being attacked from the air, as had happened in France. If invasion came to

Bristol's Regional War Cabinet. Left to right: H.M. Webb, City Engineer and ARP Controller, George Gibbs, his deputy, General Sir Hugh Elles, Regional Controller, his military advisor, and Ald. Frank Parish, Committee Chairman.

Britain, the plan was that citizens should Stay Put, and resist by being thoroughly well-organised.

Fortunately none of these plans was ever put to the test, though there was a scheme to make Bristol the scene of the first-ever rehearsal for invasion, with a massive mock invasion attack, to be carried out by troops playing the part of the Germans. The operation, code-named Thunder, proved to be too complex, and the scheme was abandoned.

One of the reasons for scrapping Thunder was a worry about the effect it would have on local morale. For almost as important as the physical preparation for war was the mental preparation: there was a propaganda war being fought as well. People's hearts and minds had to be won and this could only be done by a far-reaching campaign of exhortation and example.

At the beginning of the war, the Ministry of Information set up regional offices all over the country with two main ones for the West at Bristol and Exeter. From these offices every day streamed thousands of carefully censored news bulletins, instructions, posters and leaflets, all aimed at giving the public only the information which would keep up spirits and morale, and boost resolve to work ever harder in the war effort. 'Bad nerves' were to be discouraged.

Newspaper editors were given thousands of Defence Notices, listing subjects which they were not to mention: there were to be no weather forecasts as these would help the enemy, no hint of troop movements, no mention of factories or what they were producing, and later when the raids started, no locations of bombs, no lists of casualties, no mention of famous landmarks hit or churches or hospitals damaged. The press was not allowed to print grumbles about the queues or rationing or conscientious objectors, or shelters. There was never any printed ciriticism of the muddles caused by the local civil administrators, though plenty of it went on.

Press photographs were censored in the same way, and at daily briefings at the Ministry offices, journalists, used to spreading information, not quashing it, were told how to handle the stories of the day. Bristol became 'a West Town' and Avonmouth, designated a place of national importance, simply ceased to exist: if it was mentioned at all, it was called 'the docks area'.

The motive behind the censorship was understandable: it prevented the enemy from learning what damage they had inflicted, and kept up morale by keeping the public in ignorance. But it annoyed the readers; they felt the wool was being pulled over their eyes, as well as the enemy's, and the lack of hard information was the reason for the spread of wild rumours. Rumour-mongering was such a vice in Bristol that Anti-Rumour campaigns were run, inviting the public to sign a pledge not to spread any gossip, and to report people who did.

As it turned out, the West's newspapers could have been a source of information to the enemy; copies were regularly put on the civil aeroplanes that flew out of Whitchurch aerodrome on the Lisbon run to neutral Portugal. These planes secretly carried VIPs, royalty, heads of state and even film stars, and were much used by foreign agents on both sides.

Another means of keeping up morale was through propaganda: newsreels, films, plays, books, magazines and newspapers were vetted to see that they portrayed a Britain that was brave, cheerful, hard-working, and optimistic.

Given this efficient propaganda and censorship machine, it is not surprising that a rather one-sided image of the West's war emerged, a stiff upper lip, hearty we-can-take-it view that persisted for some years afterwards. It was not until 30 years later when classified secret documents became available, that Home Intelligence and Mass Observation reports revealed another darker side to the way people thought and felt.

Though people did take all the propaganda, from both the British and the German side, with a pinch of salt, it was nonetheless very effective: it made people think in clichés, and it managed very quickly to mythologise the war. Extremely popular in Bristol was this sample of moral uplift from Moral Re-Armament, printed on 50,000 give-away leaflets.

Morale – How You Can Play Your Part

- Forget yourself in helping your neighbours – this casts out your own fears and worries.
- Keep the moral standards of the nation high – make a break with all personal indulgences, selfishness and private wars which undermine morale and national unity.
- Be a rumour stopper – any patriot shoots rumour dead on sight.
- The secret of steadiness and inner strength is to listen to God and do what He says.
- Forearm yourself by listening to God first thing every morning – this provides a clear plan for each day.
- A British General who has fought through two wars said this: To listen to God and obey Him is the highest form of national service.

There was no explanation as to why God had told conscientious objectors that all war was wrong – but then no-one mentioned 'conchies' in those days, except with the utmost scorn, even if they did offer vainly to do war work. A team of doctors and medical students from Bristol University offered their services in the Bristol Blitz and were turned down because they were conchies, and workers at vital power stations in the West refused to work with them, in spite of the urgent need for manpower.

But more than propaganda fired the West into a new realism about what was to come. After Dunkirk, they knew it was just a matter of time. The Battle of Britain had begun, and they knew that Bristol and the West Country were full of vulnerable targets.

For there was Bristol Aeroplane Company, with its main works at Filton, and others at Corsham, Weston and Banwell, with 52,000 employees making the 'Blenheim' and later the 'Beaufort' and the 'Beaufighter'. By the end of the war, BAC was to build 2,750 aircraft, and over 100,000 engines. Equally vulnerable were Avonmouth Docks, Westlands at Yeovil, and Parnalls at Yate, where, in 1941, a lone raider came in at rooftop height and smashed the factory, which made machine gun turrets, killing 152 workers.

Shipbuilders in the West were working full out – by the end of the war they were to produce eight corvettes, 13 frigates, two boom defence vessels and many other small craft. Bristol's big engineering firms had turned to war work: Parnalls the shopfitters were making airframe components, Gardiners the ironmongers were making gun mounts, rocket launcher bases, torpedo cases, Sheldon Bush were turning out ammunition, Strachan and Henshaw, the printing machinery firm, were making submarine detection apparatus, trench mortar bombs and anti-aircraft shells, while Butler Oils made pitch for aerodrome runways, and explosives.

The very first German raid on the West, on June 20, 1940 was a flop: most of the bombs fell on the mud and shingle at Portishead, even though the Germans announced that "Bristol, one of the great trading cities has been bombed". On June 18, a plane in difficulties had shed its load of bombs on Flax Bourton, but the first raid to claim lives followed on June 25, when five people died in Bristol. On July 15 there was a raid on Westlands at Yeovil and the RNAS station at Yeovilton. The waiting game was over.

Throughout August and September 1940 there were scattered minor raids on Somerset and Bristol, but no serious incidents, so people began to relax – many of the alerts were false alarms, set off by Hitler's decoy planes, and they provided a welcome break from the relentless war work. So when the wailing up and down notes of the siren sounded in Bristol on September 25, no-one was very alarmed.

Arthur Backhurst was working at BAC, Filton, that day.

‘When the siren went, we just ambled to the shelters, thinking we'd have half an hour off and then go back to work again. There was never any sort of real urgency then.’

But in broad daylight, a perfect Y-shaped formation of 58 Heinkel bombers, escorted by 40 Messerschmitt fighters, had flown across the Channel, over Dorset and Somerset, virtually unchallenged. Their target was the BAC works at Filton.

Gerald Smith saw the planes flying over his home.

‘It was a beautiful summer's day and we heard these planes coming. We went out and looked and there was this lovely show of aircraft formation flying. I

Many lives were saved by the famous Anderson shelter: this mother and baby survived in theirs, during the daylight raid on Filton.

JF

called my sister and said look at that, and I felt intensely proud at the fine performance of the airmen. And then suddenly we realised that they had German markings! We just couldn't believe it, we thought it was a test or something . . . and then the siren went.**)**

The daylight raid on Filton was a turning point in the West's war. The simple statistics were these: 350 bombs fell in an area roughly one mile square, damaging not only the works severely, but 900 Filton and Patchway houses, and the railway line. Inside the factory complex, 72 were killed and 166 injured, of whom 19 later died. Outside the works, 58 died and 154 were seriously injured, and 11 soldiers lost their lives as they marched along the road. Those are the bald facts, but what happened that day is still indelibly etched on the minds of people who were there, like Arthur Backhurst.

❛Well, the sirens went between twenty and ten to twelve, so we locked our tool boxes and got together in groups and just ambled to the surface shelters. We started to play cards. We'd been in there about a quarter of an hour when someone came running down the shelter saying 'this one's got our number on it' and sure enough there was this terrible whistle and bang, and when it banged you had this compression feeling. I was actually lying on the blast, ten feet above the ground, I could see Patchway burning, and then I came down with a bang and one wall of the shelter fell on me and on some of my workmates, and we were trapped. We were in there a good hour until they got us out. At that stage I thought my feet had gone, I couldn't feel them. I was shouting 'get me out of here' and the man on my left was dead, and the man on my right was dead.❜

Fred Caple was in a different shelter.

❛I remember we just strolled from the factory floor, hundreds of us, and as we went to the shelters we looked up and there was this glittering, like tinfoil in the sky, something shining, dropping down, thousands of sheets of it . . . and then we all made a dive because we could actually see the bombs leaving the aircraft. We were jammed in, the bombs were raining down and we were literally being lifted inches off the floor with the blast. We could hear the clattering of the cars which were being blown on top of the shelter. I was only 19 at the time and I shall never forget it: it seemed to me that some of the older people were mumbling the Lord's Prayer.

We were all on the floor, all on top of one another, but none of us was hit. We all got out somehow and all I could think of was getting home. So I rushed out to the main gate and came upon the worst scene I've ever seen. I was literally stepping over bodies, they were being stacked up against the railings outside the works and the blood was running down the road. The bodies were of soldiers who had been marching from the Rodney works to Patchway at the time, and after the carnage I saw, I went home and was sick. It took a long time to heal me from that sight.❜

Though security was tight on the Filton raid – even now, no photographs exist to show what the destruction was like – with so many people involved, word got around the city. Gerald Smith, who in peace time worked at BAC, says:

❛Even today, not everything's been told about that raid. It's very difficult to glean any information from the survivors. And to this day I've never been able to find where the bombs actually fell. In 21 years working at the company, nobody could point to where it all happened. People just wanted to forget it.❜

At the time the Filton raid caused a great deal of anxiety and anger: how had the German planes got through without any RAF squadron being sent up to intercept them, why had there been no ack-ack barrage? Was Bristol being properly defended? And what about those surface shelters that had proved so inadequate? Bristolians began to be deeply sceptical about the safety of surface shelters and the Filton workforce from then on ignored them: when the sirens went, the work force would stream out of the works in their hundreds, on foot or bike, making for the countryside and nearby railway tunnels. The management tried to stop them, but the Filton Harriers, as they were nicknamed, literally ran for their lives.

The instant protests had their effect; when the Luftwaffe came back to bomb BAC the second time on September 27, they were met by RAF Hurricanes, and there were no casualties. But the Filton raid had shaken people's confidence. Maybe this war was not going to be so easy to win.

And the effect on that all important morale was significant. Arthur Backhurst, recovered from the injury to his feet, went back to work at BAC, a fortnight after leaving hospital.

(I went to my place and I cried because all my workmates had gone and there were strangers in their place. There were only about two millers left out of thirteen. It was devastating. I looked at the empty machines and the tears just ran down my face. I stood it all morning and then I went to the superintendent, and I was nearly in tears. He said 'can't you stand it, lad?' and I said 'no, I don't think I can.' So he sent and got my cards and my wages and I just left.)

That daylight raid on Filton on September 25, 1940, had come as a stark reminder that Britain was no longer an island, that the seas which had protected us throughout our history were no defence against air attack and that the West Country was all too vulnerable. The Luftwaffe had lost the Battle of Britain . . . now it was turning its attention to wreaking a terrible vengeance on the British people with a night-time bombing campaign that quickly introduced a chilling, menacing new word into everyday language . . . the Blitz. The great raids on London began in September 1940. By mid-November the bombers were ranging further afield to the major provincial cities. Coventry was the first to experience the horrors, then Southampton, then Birmingham. When would it be Bristol's turn?

Bristol had faced its first real baptism of fire at Filton, and already nerves were stretched too tight. But far worse was to come, as the Luftwaffe set out for Bristol on November 24 . . .

Jim Facey

2. Living through the blitz

When the city's 338th alert of the war was sounded at 6.22 p.m. on Sunday November 24, no-one took a great deal of notice. They had heard the alarms far too often to believe they warned of any great danger. It had been a quiet, dull, November Sunday.

Across the English Channel it had been foggy earlier in the day, grounding the Luftwaffe's fleet of 214 long-range bombers at their bases on the northern coast of France. But as the afternoon wore on, so the fog began to clear. The bombers could set out once more. There was a hint that conditions might become foggy once more later in the night, so the tacticians decided to limit operations to the first half of the night, choosing targets which would allow the crews ample time to return by midnight. The evening's priority: to eliminate Bristol as an important port supplying much of the Midlands and the south of England.

A fleet of 134 bombers took off to smash the heart of Bristol. The attack was to follow the by now well-established pattern perfected by the German air crews in their operations over London and elsewhere. The most experienced crews would be in the vanguard, dropping flares to pinpoint the target for their comrades. Then came showers of incendiary bombs, easily extinguishable with sand or earth, water or even the stamp of a heavy boot, but lethal in their sheer weight of numbers as they lit more and more fires, causing havoc and terror as they fell in tens of thousands. And then came the HE's, the devastatingly powerful high explosive bombs designed to rip apart buildings, shatter mains services, destroy roads and railways and disrupt fire-fighting supplies and communications. This lethal assault would leave the target in blazing chaos, a brilliantly-lit beacon for the less experienced crews to attack in later waves.

The science fiction fantasy had been of a well-drilled, close flying fleet which would arrive in perfect formation, rapidly destroy and sail home and that had, indeed, been the pattern of the tactical assault on Filton. But when it came to the strategic bombing of Britain's cities, another plan was brought into operation. This assault was even more unbearable for its victims, a hellish, seemingly endless column of enemy aircraft which came singly and at intervals of two or three minutes for hour after hour, shattering nerves and destroying hope with its sheer, inexorable relentlessness.

All of that was to come that dull November evening. Bristol had been going about its lazy, Sunday business. The centre was quiet but not deserted. Religious services were attracting large congregations at churches and halls and there were plenty of families and individuals who had been spending the day with friends or relatives and who were now making their way across the central areas by foot or on the reduced weekend bus and tram services.

Gladys Locke and her husband were at the Colston Hall, the large concert hall just off Bristol's city centre. There was always the risk of an air raid, but Bristol had seemed so peaceful and they enjoyed the Sunday night religious

Previous page: On the front line. Dazed people wander around the shattered ruins of their homes in Stafford Street, Bedminster, searching through the rubble for their possessions.

JF

services. Gladys was expecting their child.

❝My husband said, 'It's pretty safe, I don't think there'll be anything tonight', because we hadn't had any attacks for nights. So we went to the Colston Hall and we'd just got there, we were sat quite close to the organ.

I asked my husband, 'What's that noise?' It was bombs being dropped. And they announced that a raid had actually started. There was a bit of a panic and everybody tried to get out. But they wouldn't let anybody out. We sheltered under the organ and I went hysterical. A nurse came along and you know the old-fashioned way of dealing with hysterical people. She gave me a slap across the face. I wanted to get home to my mum because I knew she would be absolutely terrified. . . I was going to have a baby and I was trying to protect my baby and go and see my mother and, oh, it was terrible.❞

The first moments of the raid had transformed a blacked-out Bristol. One minute there had been darkness, the next the falling parachute flares lit up the city with a ghostly silver-white brilliance as the air hummed with the heavy drone of enemy bombers making their run-ins at 13,000 feet.

Bob Chappell had been visiting his parents in Easton when the alarm was raised and he was keen to get back to his own family as quickly as possible. His wife had given birth to their second daughter only seven days before and he didn't

The caption in the right column:

The spectral remains of one of Bristol's largest cinemas, the Regent in Clifton.

As the weeks went by, Bristolians would come to the old shopping centre around Bridge Street/Castle Street/Wine Street and stand staring at the ruins. Their morbid fascination worried the morale-watchers.

want her to be left alone with small children during an air raid. He managed to catch a tram which took him to Old Market and then he boarded a waiting bus. He watched as people came pouring from the Empire Theatre, just across the road. They had been at a concert for the congregation of St Patrick's Roman Catholic church. They hurried to the surface shelters in the middle of Old Market. Sorry, the bus conductor told Bob, the bus wouldn't be moving until the All Clear had been given. Bob decided to walk to Bedminster. He set off along Castle Street where he spotted an old school friend standing outside the Castle and Ball public house.

❛We looked up in the sky and there were bright stars. I said, 'that's flares and in a moment the whole world will be lit up like daylight and they'll drop incendiary bombs.' He asked if I'd like to go downstairs with the rest of the guests; they were all down in the cellar with the beer. But I said no. I walked through Castle Street and these incendiary bombs started coming down. The

JF

roads in those days were made of wooden blocks, tarred blocks and the bombs were falling and sticking in the wooden blocks and setting the road on fire.

So I walked up to Halfords, facing the Regent cinema, and as I stood in Halfords' doorway I could look through the glass doors of the Regent and suddenly I saw fire starting in the foyer. I thought I'd better get the hell out of there so I went past St Peter's Hospital and turned left into Bridge Street and then suddenly I heard an almighty bang from an HE. When I got down to the bottom of Bridge Street I could see that one side of the bridge was out and I could see an army of rats walking across the bridge. By that time it was quite bright because fires had started. It was incredible to see an army of rats marching across the bridge. The only thing missing was the Pied Piper standing in front.

I walked over Bristol Bridge and when I turned into Redcliffe Street I could see one tramcar on its side, one tramcar standing up straight on the rails and then behind that, about 50 yards further on, was another tramcar on its side and all the overhead wires were down. So I picked my way gingerly over the wires, not knowing whether they were live or dead. Eventually I got to St Mary Redcliffe Church. It was like daylight with all the fires. There were two surface shelters there so I entered one and pulled the sacking aside that acted like a curtain. There were two blokes sitting there scrapping and I asked what it was all about? One of them told me 'This silly bugger here was striking matches, and with an air raid on'. I said: 'Come and look outside – if you've today's *News of the World* you can put a chair outside and read it'. There were two girls there about 17 or 18, and they were breaking their hearts because they'd been caught in the raid. So I had a chat with them and we all sat down together.'

Union Street, looking up from the Odeon towards the pitiful remains of Wine Street/Castle Street, one of Jim Facey's most unforgettable images of Bristol's agony.

Passers-by gaze,
astonished, at the
surreal sight of a car
nose-dived into a
crater at the top of
Park Street.

JF

There was nothing else to do but sit, and wait . . . and hope.

Teenager Norman Allan and his friends had met in Eastville Park as they did most weekends. He'd grumbled at his mother for making tea late the previous Sunday, so this day she had made sure her boys ate early so that they could be out in the park well in time to meet the others.

‘Jerry was over before the sirens went. We were all sat round and we could hear them coming towards us as it gradually got louder and louder. Then they started dropping bombs. We were sat on the seat and my brother was next to me and as we heard the bombs falling and the flames flickering, my brother shouted at us all to get down. They all got down bar myself – I was a bit late. I felt a thud in my chest and a burning sensation. I remember lying there, my brother was with me and my friends left to go to the air raid shelter. Two girls

JF

walked towards us, two ATS girls who asked my brother if there was anything they could do. One of them put her haversack under my head as a pillow. They stayed with us. God knows how long I stayed there but it seemed an eternity. Eventually an auxiliary ambulance came collecting the injured, driven by two girls. They had to go up roads that were burning, the bombing was still going on. The flames were leaping up and they had to stop, turn round and go back. They were marvellous. Eventually we ended up at the Bristol General Hospital. I was still conscious. I remember being taken to a room and my clothes being cut off me. Then I passed out. **’**

This heavy tram was flung across the road like matchwood, landing in a shop front.

Irene Crew and her husband had been reunited the day before when he had returned home on leave from the navy. They were staying in a house near Castle Street when the air raid warning went. They hurried next door to their neighbour's shelter. Nearby was a brewery with a wine and spirit store and stables for the dray horses. Soon the air was thick with the sound of whistling, falling bombs, of the patter of countless incendiaries landing, of the crump and crash of HE's exploding and of the bangs of anti-aircraft guns. Irene and all of Bristol realised that the blitz they had so dreaded had come at last.

‘The bombs simply rained down. Every time we came up out of the shelter to see what was happening, wine bottles came over from the warehouse nearby.

JF

The flimsy buildings of the tram depot at Bedminster blown to pieces by enemy action.

The bombs dropped on the horses and sent the flesh over the wall. Each time we came out we were surrounded by parts of horses that had been blown up . . . wine, horses, you name it, it was coming at us. It was like almighty hell. You imagine a thunderstorm, you know, a real bad thunderstorm. This was just like six lots of thunder. It was terrible . . . you just can't imagine what it was like until you've been through it and got over it. ❜

The heart of this dreadful storm of fire and explosions lay around the area of Bristol Bridge but severe damage wasn't restricted to the centre of the city. Residential districts were being hit too, including Bedminster, Knowle, St George and Clifton. The city was not prepared or equipped or experienced to cope with the disaster that was now unfolding. Incendiaries kindled blaze after blaze in empty shops, offices, public buildings and homes. The bewildered, frightened full-time and part-time firemen and other emergency workers could only do their best in what rapidly became impossible circumstances.

Bill Morgan had been having tea with his mother and his future wife when his mother called him to the front door, exclaiming at 'the lovely lights in the sky' over Bristol. Bill realised just what those lovely lights meant and he hurried the two women down to the shelter. Then he donned his uniform and dashed off on his bicycle, pedalling furiously for the fire station at Brislington, about a mile-and-a-half away.

JF

‘That must have been just about the longest journey in my life. By then everything was happening, ack-ack guns blazing, incendiaries dropping everywhere. I was the only one, on a bike, in the middle of the road. I thought every bit of shrapnel, every incendiary bomb was going to hit me.’

The war brought many bizarre sights . . . schoolboys gaze at the bomb-hit wreckage of a double-decker bus in Whiteladies Road.

But he reached the fire station safely and was cheered by the companionship of his fellow fire-fighters. Bill was put in charge of a team of five men and issued with a large pump. There should have been a vehicle to tow this hefty piece of machinery, a van or at least a car, but there wasn't. Instead Bill and his firemen set off on foot, pushing the wheeled pump along the Bath Road towards the now blazing city. As they came down Kensington Hill toward's Arno's Court, a shower of incendiaries fell around them and most of Bill's men dashed off with shovels and spades to dig the flaming bombs into whatever ground they could find. That left Bill and another man desperately clinging to the hefty pump. They couldn't control it and the pump gathered momentum as it ran down the hill, the two men clinging on for dear life. Somehow they managed to steer it into the kerb. An HE landed nearby and the two were showered with masonry and earth but were unhurt. A passing fire crew spotted the pump, commandeered it at once and towed it away by car to help other firemen who were fighting a blaze at a nearby uniform factory. Bill was left with just a stirrup pump and a bucket while all around him Bristol blazed. He still managed to save one row of deserted houses when he spotted an incendiary alight in one of them. He ran in and put out the fire in the smoke-filled building.

Shortly afterwards Bill and his team were picked up by a large van combing the area, collecting as many firemen as possible for the fight for the city. Every available man was needed to save central Bristol. They were left at Redcliffe Street amidst awe-inspiring scenes of devastation.

‘They had big Beresford pumps on the harbour and they were pumping gallons and gallons of water but the unpreparedness of it all showed then. The hose was an old canvas one and it was so full of holes that we had as much water coming out of the holes as we did from the nozzle. Somebody got hold of a load of tin baths and they were placed along the hose – you could hear the ping-pong-ping-pong as the water was coming out.

When you're fighting a fire with HE bombs falling around you, there's so much damage that all you can really hope to do is to put the fire out quick enough to stop it becoming a target for the next load of bombers. There was no hope of saving buildings, not when there was exploding bombs as well. Anybody who said they weren't frightened, they weren't heroes, they were nuts. I felt terror-stricken, absolutely frightened to death, but you got used to it.’

Bill Graves, serving in the ARP, was having just as dramatic a night in the Wine Street/Castle Street area on the other side of the river. He had been sent to St Peter's Hospital, one of the finest remaining Tudor mansions in the country, to help rescue monuments and archives from the already blazing buildings.

‘We were getting out chairs and bits and pieces when the ARP guy in charge pulled us back and suddenly we looked up and the lead on the roof of St Peter's Church and St Peter's Hospital had melted. It was starting to roll towards the river, like a silver stream. It was beautiful, there's no other expression for it, but it was dreadful. Then I was ordered to close off the bottom of Castle Street and the road was on fire.

After it had been closed off a green ambulance came down with a girl driving. She was only about 19, not much older than me. She asked me where the Central Health Clinic was, which was just down below where we were. They were still taking the casualties down there even though there was fire all around. This girl was as cool as a cucumber, and she had just come through Dante's *Inferno.*’

It was an inferno that was by now raging unchecked. There were more than 70 large fires, many of which needed at least five pumps to fight them. But Bristol only had 224 appliances available. The city didn't have the manpower either. The fire brigade was under strength by 77 men with 995 full-time firemen in service. That was enough to man 96 appliances. The remaining appliances were being manned, wherever possible, by 897 part-time firemen. It was an equation with one inevitable, deadly outcome. . . Bristol became a city of flames.

Besides the firemen, desperately trying to cope against such impossible odds, there was the grim work of trying to rescue people trapped in fallen masonry and then take them to safety. Bristol's ARP teams worked throughout the height of the raid, rescuing 137 people as bombs and fires raged around them. There were many, many individual cases of heroism by the men and women who

King Street, one of Bristol's most historic streets. Despite the firemen's efforts, these houses (foreground) were lost but the Llandoger Trow beyond was saved.

JF

worked throughout that night and these heroes of the blitz paid dearly. This first Bristol blitz claimed the lives of eight firemen, 22 ARP wardens, two ARP messenger boys and two ambulance drivers.

To those fighting fires, rescuing the injured, treating the casualties or hiding in whatever shelters they could find, the raid seemed to last forever but finally, shortly after 11 p.m., the last drone of the last bomber's engines died away. It was over. As the German crews crossed the English Channel on the final leg of their journey back to base, they could look back to see a clear, bright red glow on the clouds many miles away. Below that glow, Bristol was burning. Shortly before midnight, the long, clear, steady note of All Clear was sounded.

After an ordeal that had lasted without respite for almost four hours, the people of Bristol emerged from their hiding places to survey the scene. They found that the order of an ancient English city had been reduced to chaos and anarchy.

JF

The bottom of Bridge Street. The day before this had been Bristol's most popular shopping centre. It has never been rebuilt and gutted St Peter's Church still stands roofless, a memorial to the night of the first great Bristol blitz.

Irene Crew and her husband had survived some of the most intense bombing. They could hardly believe what they saw.

❝Oh gosh, everything was flattened. There was water everywhere, all the pipes burst, kids crying, parents trying to find their children . . . chaos.❞

Across the city centre at the Colston Hall, Gladys Locke and her husband were at last allowed to leave. The building was unscathed and she was anxious to hurry off to her mother's home in Brislington as quickly as possible.

❝The walk through the city was, well, I don't think anybody could describe it. There were buildings falling down, there were rescue operations going on with all the people buried, there was water gushing in the streets, there were gas mains going. You had to pick your way through where you could get through. But there were fires and the smell of gas and people shouting and screaming. And crowds of people huddled about with blankets over them and ambulances running here, there and everywhere. It was terrible.❞

Gladys and her husband struggled through the rubble-littered streets and made the long, weary trudge to her mother's home to find her sheltering in the coal house, terrified but unhurt.

The tottering remains of the Dutch House, one of the saddest architectural losses of the war. What was left was pulled down shortly after this picture was taken.

JF

When dawn broke, daylight offered a dismal scene. Smoke still rose from the debris, there were flickers of flame from remaining fires and the air was heavy with the choking, bitter smell of scorched timber and masonry. The streets were filthy with blackened water from the night's fire-fighting efforts and glass lay everywhere.

People wandered about, numbed by the sight of so many familiar landmarks reduced to smoking piles of rubble. More than 10,000 homes had been damaged. Factories had been hit. Churches destroyed. Some of the city's finest architectural heritage had vanished in the night or been left in ruins. The Dutch House was a skeleton, St Peter's Church and St Peter's Hospital damaged beyond repair. With them had gone Bristol's most popular, favourite shopping centre in the busy streets around Wine Street and Castle Street. This was where the weekending promenaders and window-shoppers used to gather in their

JF

Powerful high-explosive bombs and a hail of incendiaries left Wine Street a scene of dreadful devastation.

thousands. Now it was a city of the dead. It took some days before the actual death toll could be counted and then the final tally was 207 killed, 187 seriously injured and another 703 slightly injured. Almost 1,400 had been made homeless and water, gas and electricity supplies had all been badly disrupted.

There was an ominous silence that morning, broken by the crack of falling masonry, the drip of water, the crunch of footsteps on fragments of broken glass. It was a silence that was echoed by the press.

At the very time Bristolians were desperate for information, they were given none. The crack-down on news was almost total. People wanted to know which parts of town had been hit, which had been spared. How many had died? Which famous buildings had been destroyed in the raid? The censor forbade all answers. That Monday's *Evening Post* carried a terse seven paragraphs on the horrors of the night before. "It was stated" the report read, "that the casualties were comparatively few." Another brisk, morale-boosting line read that "the men of the fire and ARP services performed stupendous labours in bringing the fires under contol". These pathetically censored reports briefly amused, then angered readers.

Worse was to follow. If people couldn't believe what they saw in the papers, at least they could trust with their own eyes what they saw on the newsreels. The British Movietone report on the attack was watched with the closest interest . . . and growing disbelief. The item on the Bristol blitz spoke of a

JF

Park Street, the morning after, the pavements littered with glass, rubble and burnt timbers. The acrid smell of destruction hung in the air.

cheery and defiant Bristol. It was 'business as usual' despite the worst that Hitler could do. The film showed no damage at all. That was hardly surprising. The scenes of Bristol flashed across the screen were out of date – they had been taken three months before the night of November 24.

Bristol was never mentioned by name in the reports. It was slyly referred to as 'A Town In The West', a silly, useless cloak of anonymity which didn't fool anyone, least of all the German propaganda machine which was quickly announcing that "as a distribution centre and important railway junction, Bristol has been wiped out". All the British learnt was that a 'Town In The West' had suffered some sort of damage but that casualties were 'comparatively few'. It took some time before people realised that the truth lay somewhere between the two.

There was another, insidious effect of that petty official refusal to tell Britain about the Bristol blitz. Weeks before, Coventry had been hailed as a city of national heroes for its citizens' courage and endurance under the fire of enemy bombing. Bristolians received no such recognition, no such sympathy and no such place in the canons of World War II. Seeds of resentment were sown that first day and the bitterness they caused would last for many years.

When the first feelings of shock had died away, the criticisms quickly followed. The fire services came in for bitter complaints. Too many people had had to endure the ordeal of watching their homes or workplaces, local shops or

JF

The buckled remains of St Philip's Bridge after it was struck. neighbourhood landmarks burn down without any apparent effort to stop the flames. There were also noisy complaints about Bristol's seemingly useless defences against air attack. Certainly the anti-aircraft artillery efforts that night had hardly been reassuring. The bombers had come, bombed at will and departed without check. There was dismay at press censorship. The resentment, the lack of information and the hardships and worries made Bristol a fertile breeding ground for rumour and rancour.

But there was another, positive side to Bristol's reaction to that first big raid. It came from comradeship in disaster, a shared sense of loss, a new team spirit. Home Intelligence, which was keeping a close watch on civilian reaction to blitz raids, took note of all the grumbles but concluded that Bristol's morale was good and that the city had taken the blow on the chin. There was grim determination in this moment of adversity.

The report stated: "The citizens took the blow almost light heartedly at first. Co-operation and practical good neighbourliness limited dislocation to a great extent. But by the 28th, when people were becoming tired from their exertions, when the lack of water here or gas there and transport difficulties nearly everywhere became increasingly irksome, this mood became more serious. The fact remains that the people of the West Country are stout hearted and without thought of surrender".

Nothing would be the same again. Bristol never took an air raid warning

lightly after that black Sunday. From then, when the sirens sounded, most people took shelter as quickly as they could. There were a few bright spirits, usually in the more distant suburbs, who refused to take any notice of air raids and carried on throughout the worst of the blitzes as if nothing more exciting than a fireworks display was going on outside. They took a cheerfully fatalistic view of it all. If your number was up, so be it. But these were rarities, and they were almost always protected by distance from the main target of the damaged inner city.

Bristol Bridge. The skyline would never be the same after the first great raid.

The November 24 attack was followed by a raid on the docks at Avonmouth, but then the bombers headed for other targets, London, Liverpool, Birkenhead, Plymouth and, significantly, Southampton. The November 24 raid had been preceded by an attack on Southampton.

On a bitterly cold night on Monday December 2, the bombers returned to Bristol. It was a re-run of that first night of the blitz. The sirens sounded at 6.18 p.m., the anti-aircraft guns began pounding two minutes later and then came the blinding flares to light up the city followed by showers of incendiaries and then the crash of HEs. The main target was the central area of the city, once again, but there was also damage in St George, Knowle, Brislington, Cotham and Redland.

The emergency services, men and women, were often heroic in the face of the terror and destruction that surrounded them. A contemporary account of one

JF

Putting a good face on things. The Duke of Kent on a morale-boosting visit to wrecked Castle Street . . . the kind of picture the censor was happy to approve for use in the press.

woman ARP warden's shift that dreadful night reveals the full extent of the ordeals they faced.

❦ She had been on duty since 10 a.m. when the night raid began. She first assisted a woman who was buried up to her neck, gave her a cup of tea and stood by for half an hour helping in the rescue work. Unfortunately that woman she had helped subsequently died. The woman warden then rescued a small boy and handed him to the First Aid party. Continuing her search for victims, she found a foot protruding from the rubble. After removing the debris, the headless body of a man was found. Then, on hearing that a baby was missing, she searched the area, found the child and restored it to the mother. Afterwards she came upon a woman whose husband had been killed and whose four children were missing. She comforted the woman and found out where her children were. Numerous dead bodies were collected and covered up by her during her duties, while all the time the bombs were falling. She was instructed at 8.30 a.m. the following morning to leave her duty and obtain some rest, but she refused and carried on for some hours more. ❧

That raid cost 156 lives with another 149 people seriously injured. Services were very badly disrupted. Once again the cold weather made life in the many damaged homes that much more wretched.

JF

The assault ground on. Blitz, chaos, attempts to clear up and clean up and then blitz again. The Luftwaffe were back in force over Bristol for the third time in less than a fortnight on Friday December 6. The raid killed 100, seriously injured 80 and caused yet another crack in a morale that was already tottering from so much punishment. People had become obsessed with shelter and safety from bombs. Sirens sent the jumpy population racing for cover and sunset in those early evenings of winter became a time of dread and foreboding for most people. Many did not even wait for the sirens to shriek out – they had begun a daily routine of seeking out somewhere they believed to be safe long before nightfall came.

For most Bristolians, night meant bedding down in whatever local shelter was available. The better off, particularly in the suburbs, had long since installed Anderson shelters in their gardens. Some went one better, digging deep refuges under their gardens, complete with all sorts of comforts, carpets, good bunks, food, candles and pictures on the wall.

The poorer folk flocked to the communal surface shelters, but these quickly lost their reputation as safe refuges when bombs began falling. And for the very good reason that they offered precious little protection if a bomb fell close by. It wasn't long before many people had heard of incidents like the one Bob Chappell witnessed after bombs fell on Bedminster.

The Duke of Kent gazes at the remains of what had been Woolworth's store in Castle Street.

The shape of things to come, this tenement building in the Horsefair was the first house to be bombed and destroyed in Bristol.

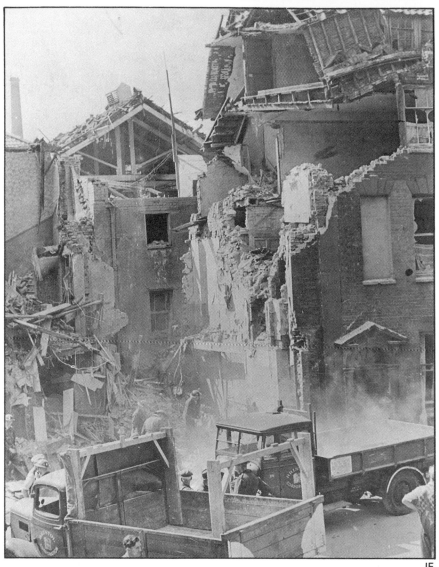

JF

‘We used to have surface shelters in the streets for local people. On that occasion, I could see that the roof of this shelter had shifted about, well, let's say a foot. It wasn't on square and when I looked inside it was full of people sat side by side all the way round and everyone was dead. They had their eyes open and it was just as if they were sitting there not seeing anything. It was the blast from the bomb. It hadn't affected the shelter, only shifted the roof, but the blast killed them.’

The deeper the safer, that was what people began to believe and it became an obsession. It was as if the city wanted to burrow further and further underground to hide from the horrors above. People hunted out refuges wherever they could in spite of official warnings that many of the so-called 'safe' places could prove death traps if they suffered a direct hit from an HE.

They went down into the ancient crypts of old churches, they re-discovered abandoned coal workings and railway tunnels, they sought safety in Redcliffe caves and, most notorious of all, they flocked to the 525-foot-long Portway tunnel under Bridge Valley Road in the Avon gorge. No amount of hectoring from the authorities could prevent nightly crowds arriving on the Portway. The tunnel won a rumoured reputation as the one truly safe place to spend a night at the height of a blitz, and thousands wanted their share of that safety. They filed down from middle-class homes in Clifton, they traipsed across the Avon and the New Cut from Ashton and Bedminster and they plodded along the Portway from Hotwells and Sea Mills.

Gerald Smith:

❛We thought we'd be the only ones going there. So we trekked down from our house at about 4 p.m. It was a dark, cold, winter evening. We got down to the tunnel and there must have been 700 or 800 people. It was absolute chaos. Everyone was trying to get to the tunnel . . . fear had now taken over because the bombing was so dreadful. We didn't arrive first – we probably arrived almost last. And because we were the last, fortunately we were at the end of the tunnel. The others had jam-packed themselves in. It was terrible. They were fighting for places.

You couldn't lay out. You stood or knelt, cooped up with your back against the wall, and it was always streaming with water. We couldn't sleep. Sleep was almost impossible. Any sleeping was done during the day, either in school or at home. Because there were no doors, you couldn't close it off and people would arrive during the night, especially when a raid was taking place. It was sheer panic.❜

Officials who visited the tunnel found a stinking, damp-sodden nightmare of a place, littered with the debris of weeks of dossing. Yet at the worst times, it was estimated that as many as 3,000 people attempted to squeeze into the tunnel to escape the dangers outside. The public health hazards became so great that the authorities had to act. The police were sent in to clear the place of shelterers. The tunnel was thoroughly cleansed and, eventually 400 ticket-holders granted refuge there each night. Those who had been ejected and were then banned from further use of the tunnel resented their removal bitterly.

If there was no more room in the Portway tunnel, people soon found underground alternatives. Old pit workings in east Bristol were a magnet to many local people who showed a pathetic belief in their safety. A direct hit would almost certainly have buried any shelterers in tons of choking coal dust, slack and rock, too deep for any rescue operation. Schoolgirl June O'Connor took nightly refuge in a disused coal train tunnel near her home.

❛The sirens would start and Mum would get us ready with a bottle of water and bread and jam and our coat or blanket and perhaps a pillow and off we would go. People came from miles around and you'd see them scurrying through the tunnel to get to their favourite place which they'd probably had for weeks and weeks. We would feel terribly cold as we lay down with our coats over us, but we would hear the guns at Purdown and all the bombing above us.

We were cold and frightened so all the strangers used to comfort us and sometimes cuddle us and they would sing songs to try to cheer us up and to help pass the night away. It was really cold. But because there were so many people crammed in this tunnel, it sort of contained our body heat. The walls were terribly damp and you could see all the fungi on the walls and the water dripping down. In the morning we would emerge from the tunnel and collect all the shrapnel that had fallen. It was a sort of trophy. Yes, we were tired and I can remember going to school and falling asleep on my desk because we had had so many broken nights' sleep. I don't think the teachers minded too much because everybody around us had experienced the same sort of restless nights. We just accepted it, we just thought it was a way of life. We could see no end to it. It was just something that went on and on. **)**

The forbidden listening to the broadcasts from Germany by William Joyce, nicknamed Lord Haw-Haw, became very common. One told a Mass Observation researcher that Haw-Haw gave the same news as the BBC, only days sooner. Gerald Smith can remember the broadcasts.

(He obviously knew Bristol well – some say he once lived in Clifton. He used to say, 'Watch out you people tonight, we're coming over' and, sure enough, they did. I remember a new building in Stokes Croft, Blundells, and Lord Haw-Haw said 'Tonight we're going to hit one of your favourite stores, Blundells' and, blow me, they did hit it. But people really took him as a joke with his 'Germany calling'. You just listened to him because of his cheek. **)**

Those sleepless nights in congested, damp, underground places, those daily sirens and that grinding background of fear took its toll. Morale began to plummet. People were worried and angry at the lack of safe shelters, bitter at what they felt was civic tardiness and ineptitude in clearing up the mess of the raids and increasingly defeatist in their attitude towards the war. Some chilling quotes were recorded by Mass Observers trying to gauge Bristol's mood. "Of course we're losing, we're only one little country". "Why don't we call an armistice?"

The report concluded: "Morale in Bristol is being left to drift in its own direction far too much and there is a dangerous lack of imaginative leadership and especially a rather poor quality of local leadership in this area. It would seem quite possible that depression and defeatist feelings which at present only exist in embryo might heavily and quite rapidly increase in Bristol unless something is done to give the people positive feelings of pride and purpose".

All very well, but what Bristol needed most was a respite from the great air raids. A decent night's sleep and an evening or two without the dreaded air raid siren would have worked far greater miracles than any imaginative leadership, local or otherwise. It wasn't to be. The sirens went regularly and the only mercy was that there was a lull from the big blitzes. Throughout this period the voluntary welfare workers and other services set a remarkable example with their help and their cheerfulness. They couldn't keep the bombers away but they could – and did – do their best to help and to restore crushed spirits as Christmas approached. There was food for shelterers, assistance for the homeless, immediate, practical help for the direct victims of the raids. People responded to their example and whenever, for example, the Red Cross made appeals for blood donors, there was never a lack of willing volunteers. Things even began to improve in some of the worst shelters and Christmas night wasn't the miserable occasion it might have been.

Gerald Smith:

(It was better in the Portway tunnel. We even had a Primus stove and could

JF

cook a little meal. And people were very genuine. You could leave everything where it was and nobody touched it. There was a lot of comradeship. We all got to know one another, we'd have a singalong.

But the fear was that we were going to have a raid on Christmas night. People would say that the enemy wouldn't do that; there were people saying the enemy would. This apprehension marred Christmas to start with. We went down the tunnel early Christmas Day because it was dark at 4 o'clock. We decorated as best we could, we made some paper chains and put them on the wall. Of course they all fell down because the wall was wet. There were rations for Christmas pudding, so mother boiled up some pudding. I had a little tramways conductor's set. My sister had a knitted doll and I had a comic and we thought it was fabulous. And then people started swapping. If you hadn't got any nuts, somebody else gave you some and you didn't have any cake, somebody gave you and you gave and they gave. **'**

Devastation in Cheriton Place, Henleaze. Although the inner city took the brunt of the blitzes, the suburbs suffered damage too.

And so 1940 drew to a close without a further big-scale bombing assault, although some bombs did fall on the city and nightly fly-pasts of enemy aircraft on their way to other targets further inland ensured continual air raid warnings and yet more sleepless nights. The weather, already cold, grew ominously colder in a city of broken windows, damaged buildings and disrupted public services. And then the Luftwaffe returned in force.

JF

The pathetic remains of bombed properties in South Street, Bedminster.

On the evening of Friday, January 3 1941, people heard the hated drone of enemy bombers heading towards Bristol once again. It was the start of what developed into one of the longest air raids experienced anywhere at this stage of the World War II. The sirens sounded at 6.21 p.m. and, as the attack began, the city's heavy anti-aircraft artillery went into action. Then, after just 10 minutes, the sound of the Bristol guns died away. Bristolians listening from their shelters couldn't understand what had gone wrong and why bombs were falling without answering fire from our guns. They might have been reassured if they had known the answer. Air Intelligence had learnt several hours before that Bristol was to be the target of another blitz, and this time the RAF wanted to give its night fighters a chance to beat the bombers. So, as the first enemy aircraft approached, night-flying Hurricanes were scrambled and all anti-aircraft artillery ordered to shut down to give the Hurricanes a free rein to attack the Germans. As things turned out, the fighters did nothing to stem the assault during their allotted hour over Bristol while the silent guns angered and frightened the people shivering in whatever shelters they could find on that sub-zero night. Hopes that this might be a short raid were raised when an All Clear sounded at 8.59 p.m.

Moreen Sellers was one of many thousands who sighed with relief when she heard that All Clear. She had been sheltering under the stairs of her Bedminster home with her brother, mother and grandmother. Her father, who worked for

JF

the tramways company, was away at work. The next day was to be her brother's ninth birthday. As the All Clear died away, her mother left their cupboard refuge to make some tea while her grandmother went to sit by the fire to warm herself against the cold. She took the children's socks with her and hung them in front of the fire. Within a couple of minutes, the air raid sirens were howling again.

'The German bombers hadn't gone away, they were still over Bristol. My brother and I put on the warm socks and went back into the cupboard. We had beds there under the stairs. Mother was making tea in the scullery and the lights went out. Mother dropped everything and dived under the dining room table. It was all quiet. It seemed such a long time that I was waiting for something to happen and suddenly I could hear this sort of soft crackle in the roof and it grew louder and louder and then it all came down on us. All the dust and the smell of the smoke around us and my grandmother shouting 'Oh help, oh God help me'. The stairs took the weight of a lot of it, the roof and the furniture and things that were upstairs. Then everything was all quiet and it was all dusty and horrible. It seemed an eternity to me. My brother and I had our heads sort of stuck and we couldn't move. It wasn't hurting but we couldn't move and then, after a long, long time we heard some men saying 'Don't worry, we'll get you out, don't panic'.'

"Knocked about a bit in Bedminster", Jim Facey wrote on the back of this picture. Sailors and other servicemen joined in the big clear-ups which followed each raid.

JF

A scene reminiscent of the nightmare landscapes of the Western Front in World War I . . . blitzed Bedminster.

They were moving things and digging and pushing things away and they got my brother and me out and took us to the air raid shelter at E.S. and A. Robinson, quite near. I didn't know what had happened to my mother; then I heard she had been taken away with my grandmother in a lorry with tarpaulin over the top. No-one spoke to us in the shelter. We knew they lived in the area, so they should have said hullo, like you speak to children, but I suppose they were all concerned with their own homes. They knew we'd been bombed and they lived near us, so I suppose they got frightened thinking what they'd find when they got out.

The All Clear went. My brother started crying. He said 'What are we going to do?' and I said, 'Don't worry about it, we'll take you down to Auntie Winn's and Uncle Bob's', my mother's brother. We began walking, in the middle of the road. My father always said that if you've got to go out after an air raid, then walk in the middle of the road because you'll be away from falling slates and things from roofs and incendiary bombs in shop doorways or gardens. My brother kept saying, 'Who's going to look after us?' and I told him not to worry, that I was his big sister. And I was only a year and 11 months older than him. It was just lucky, my uncle came towards us and asked what we were doing. So of course I broke down and cried and told him that Gran and Mum had been taken away and I didn't know where. He took us in and said he'd find Mummy and Grandma when it was light. **'**

JF

Meanwhile Moreen's father, who had spent a busy night helping to drive as many buses as possible out of Bristol to the safety of the countryside so that the city would have public transport once the blitz was over, had arrived home to find his house destroyed and his family missing.

❝He had thought we were all dead underneath all that rubble. He walked into my aunt's house and saw us and we ran into his arms and we all cried together, we just cried and cried and cried. My two uncles went all around Bristol to all the hospitals and found my mother but my grandmother had died.❞

The sights Bristol was forbidden to see by the censor, the dead hastily covered by sheets after a raid on Easton.

Moreen's mother survived. Her vision was badly affected by the shock and blast of the direct hit and her eyes remained bandaged for many weeks. Gradually her eyesight recovered but the family's nerves were gone, shattered by their ordeal. Before long they found refuge in Chewton Mendip, outside Bristol and away from the bombing.

The final, true All Clear sounded at 6.21 a.m., exactly 12 hours after the initial warning. The raid had been savage, as Bristol discovered in the light of dawn. More than 180 aircraft had been sent to pound Bristol and only 14 failed to reach the target. To make matters worse for the emergency services trying to cope with the disaster, the severe cold badly hampered fire-fighting, with water rapidly freezing in the open air. The centre of Bristol, Bedminster, Knowle and

JF

Clearing the debris in Stokes Croft. The disruption and the devastation of repeated raids soon sapped morale.

Clifton all suffered hits. About 2,500 houses were damaged and 149 people were killed, 133 seriously injured and more than 200 slightly hurt.

Gerald Smith and his brothers and sisters were handed food and hot drinks by the Salvation Army when they emerged from the shelter of the Portway tunnel that bleak January morning.

Their walk home through the streets of a blitzed Bristol was a terrible experience for Gerald and so many other children who witnessed the results of a protracted air raid.

‘When we got to the main street near our home, all the houses were caved in on the street. There were hose pipes, dogs barking, sirens going, burglar alarms sounding, an absolute cacophony of war. When we got to what we thought was our street, there were many corpses laid on the corner of the pavement and the pavement was sloping, up to the houses. I remember blood was running from the bodies into the main road and this went on down the road, as if somebody was tipping buckets of red paint. We saw people walking along with parts of torsos, matching them with shoes or coats, piecing them together, which was very distressing. We talked about it among ourselves that first day. When we went to school, we said, ‘What have you seen?’ In the end, we became so hardened we could talk about our daily scan of what we’d seen and be competitive about it and, of course, things did get out of proportion.’

JF

The bombers' legacy . . . the poignant columns of the Arcade, Broadmead.

The memories of those first days of 1941 are of fear, fatigue and, above all, of cold. Bill Graves was one of tens of thousands of Bristolians who suffered the deprivations of surviving one of the worst winters on record in a damaged home.

❛The cold was really numbing, it was debilitating. It pulled you down. My grandparents had been bombed out and they were living with us. Their bomb had fallen fairly close to us so all our windows were out. We had bits of tar paper whacked in – unless your roof was off, nobody bothered, you had to soldier on. The wind blew through the tar paper and through every crack and crevice. Coal wasn't easy to come by so where they'd pulled the wooden blocks up out of the road, we'd gather them in a sack or on a cart and take them to burn at home. I remember seeing dozens of people with cars full of old blocks. They had

JF

The weather of the first days of 1941 was so cold that water froze in hosepipes as Bristol firemen tried to fight the raging blazes. The intense cold caused misery to tens of thousands in damaged, windowless, unheated homes.

nothing else to burn.

Our house had its windows blown and the front door blown and we didn't see anybody official. You sent in a card to say your house was damaged and eventually they sent someone to look, officials from the ARP and they'd write down details on a sheet of paper. People got fed up with how long it took, and the cold . . . and everything else. **'**

Tess Broughton has equally bitter memories of those January days.

' There was a blitz and we were without heat and water for about two weeks at our home in Bishopston. You just shivered or wrapped yourself well up in what you could find, blankets and things like that. Coal was hardly available, and we were starving. We just didn't get enough to eat and you never saw a fat woman during the war. Then we had an open fire and we used to cook on that and on a little sixpenny meths stove. But there was no water for bathing or anything like that. We did cope until everything was put back on. **'**

The poor suffered badly in a Bristol disrupted by repeated blitz attacks. Betty Screen's family survived on the charity of neighbours in the worst times.

' We had bread pudding, we had the ends of loaves that neighbours didn't want, they sent that up. And large tins of baked potatoes – that was the favourite, when neighbours sent over large tins of baked potatoes.

There was one time we sat down and cried. Mum told us that she was sorry, but there was no food for us. And suddenly a knock would come at the door and it might be half a loaf. So Mum used to cut it into thick pieces and then cut it into very large, thick fingers and we used to suck the bread to make it last. I know it sounds incredible but that's what we actually did. We used to suck the bread to make it last before we went to bed. **'**

The 12-hour ordeal of the fourth great attack that Friday was followed by another raid the following evening, but this did not develop into a full-scale blitz. Fires broke out in Avonmouth and Bristol and the cold made fire-fighting doubly difficult. Bill Morgan was called out at 4 a.m. to deal with a blaze in Victoria Street, near the Shakespeare public house.

'The hoses were all along the gutters and they were frozen solid. You just couldn't move for ice and everything was festooned with icicles. Your clothing got frozen up. I got my fiancée to knit me a blue balaclava and I put that on and put the steel helmet on top of that and the balaclava froze to my face – it was like a solid piece around my face. **'**

Turntable ladders were immobilised by ice. Blow lamps had to be used to free equipment from the grip of ice. Great icicles hung from roofs and ladders as the firemen worked and they posed a nasty threat to the crews below, icy spears which might come hurtling down without any warning. Pumps froze and the roads became skating rinks, a hazard both to vehicles and fire teams on foot. The cold was so bitter by now that a cup of hot tea would rapidly turn to ice if left unattended for any time. And for the injured, trapped in bombed buildings, there was the added ordeal of icy water landing on them and freezing as firemen led the way to save them from the flames.

But the raids died away and at last the weather changed. Warmer air arrived and the conditions became mild and damp. The weather offered a double bonus, relief from the cold and the protection of thick clouds over Bristol. Heavy rain in Northern France waterlogged the runways and the Luftwaffe's operations were severely hampered.

This change was sorely needed. Bristol was desperate for some respite from front line action. The nightly cramming together in damp, unhygienic shelters had brought illness and epidemics, with a high incidence of bronchitis and pneumonia among the weakened population. There were the day-to-day problems of life in a city from which so many fathers and husbands were absent, in which considerable numbers of children were running wild in the streets because schools had been damaged or destroyed. There was the struggle for survival in cold, windowless, cheerless homes. And there was the grinding terror of waiting for the next blitz attack.

At the dawn of Spring, 1941 Mass Observation tested the mood of Bristol. The report of March 3 noticed that the raiders' absence and the warmer weather had had positive results despite the deprivations being suffered by many. Surface morale was 'reasonably good', with less signs of the 'shaky morale' which had caused so much concern in the wake of the first blitzes. Bristolians were even finding time to grumble at Bristol City Council – an age-old sport – for its inadequacies, this time in clearing up all the mess. There was a great deal of annoyance about what many felt was the foolish storage of highly-prized foodstuffs in warehouses which were easy prey to enemy bombers. People spoke of great mountains of cheese and maramalade stored in the Bristol area . . . and everyone longed for cheese and marmalade. But, Mass Observation remarked, 'food supplies are adequate'. The report noted with relief that the cinemas were doing good business and that concerts and meetings were well attended. A new spirit of comradeship had emerged. There had been 'an appreciable post-blitz levelling of class distinction in some districts, particularly Knowle'. It was attributed largely to the method of fire watching . . . 'fire watchers get together in groups and go to one another's houses in turns. The atmosphere is generally a social one'.

The eviction of hundreds from the Portway Tunnel still rankled, the tip of an iceberg of discontent about the refuges available during an air raid. The report said: 'half of this shelter had been forcibly cleared by the police as it was necessary to avoid infection. Truncheons were reported to have been used and there was some bad feeling about this. There is a continuance of dissatisfaction with shelters, Andersons being flooded and there being few deep shelters. Surface shelters are generally held in disrepute.'

On Sunday March 16 1941 the fragile peace was shattered by the deadliest Bristol blitz of the war. Weather conditions had improved for the Luftwaffe crews and the chosen targets were Avonmouth and the city docks. The raid lasted from 8.27 p.m. to 4.15 a.m. and the 162 bombers which took part caused terrible damage around Temple Meads and Lawrence Hill. Bombs fell on surrounding areas including Easton and Eastville, Whitehall, St Pauls and Montpelier, Knowle, Fishponds and the Cotham/Redland/Clifton area. The casualty figures were the worst suffered in any of the Bristol blitzes: 257 people killed and another 391 badly hurt. The raid reached its terrifying crescendo when a gas holder exploded, sending a jet of flame shooting more than 3,000 feet into the air in a blinding red glare.

Ernest Smith was among the injured that night. He was caught off-guard by what proved to be a false All Clear signal at about 1 a.m. When he heard the steady note signalling that the danger was passed, he left home to make his way to the NAAFI at Broad Plain to see what he could do to help post-blitz operations. He pulled on wellington boots and donned his steel helmet before setting off. He did not get very far. The air raid sirens howled and as he walked down the road a shower of flares and incendiaries sent him to cover in the nearest communal shelter. He recognised many neighbours as he glanced around.

‘As I got inside this shelter, round the corner, I heard this bomb screaming down and I went flat on my face. I thought this was it. I couldn't have been unconscious all that long, probably 10 minutes, quarter of an hour. And when I came round, my head was spinning, my ears were ringing. And I had a wonderful feeling of being alive. I stumbled over bodies. There were about 20 people killed in there. I knew them personally. I spoke to Mr Osborne who was there and he said 'My legs are gone' and I put his arms around my shoulders and we got into the entrance. We found Mr Stone lying in the entrance. He'd been out to make a tray of tea because of that quarter hour break with the All Clear and then the sirens went again. He had been caught in the entrance carrying the tray of tea.’

Ernest Smith managed to carry Mr Osborne away from the ruined shelter to a cellar refuge across the road. He recognised more neighbours.

‘They knew the people that had been in the street shelter with us and Mrs Stone was there. She asked about her husband – and he was the one lying in the entrance. And I couldn't really tell her at the time. I couldn't bring myself to tell her that her husband had been killed.’

Mr Osborne did not survive his injuries either. He died later in hospital. Ernest Smith was taken to the casualty department which had been set up at the Bristol Eye Hospital. He was treated for his injuries and told he was lucky to be alive after a direct hit. When he was well enough, he was sent away to the seaside to recover from the shock. He has suffered from claustrophobia ever since.

This raid, which followed two months of relative calm, had a devastating effect on local people. Nerves were stretched to breaking point and there was fury at the sounding of a false All Clear. Mass Observation made its third report shortly after the attack and the observers were shocked at what they discovered.

Sections of the report read:

‘A large proportion of people are definitely nervy. Bad talk and general complaints against the war have distinctly increased. The big raid on Sunday March 16 has done more to upset morale in Bristol than any two of the previous raids put together. People are getting worn out with the continual bombardment in a place where every bomb is a bomb somewhere quite near you and at you (none of the anonymity of London or the other major cities). The irregular, sporadic, sudden switching of heavy raids here has a strongly disturbing effect.’

People were worn out by the mess and deprivations which followed each raid. They had little confidence in Bristol's anti-aircraft guns – the raiders seemed to

The Luftwaffe attacked Bristol because it was seen as a major distribution and transport centre. But despite damage like this near Temple Meads, the blitzes failed to destroy the transport system.

A coach cut in half by the force of falling masonry.

come and go as they pleased, delivering body blows to Bristol and escaping scot-free. They were furious about false All Clear signals which had cost many lives in mid-raid. They were becoming convinced – and not without reason – that seaports were now the main target for the German bombers and that Bristol would never be allowed lasting peace.

The greatest burdens fell, inevitably, on the poorer citizens. They were the ones living in the central areas receiving the brunt of the aerial assault. They had no cars to escape the blitzes. There was no money for small luxuries to comfort themselves. Their voices weren't loud enough to attract attention from the authorities. Those living in the better-off suburbs were not only better fed, more mobile and, usually, better equipped with stout domestic shelters – they were also two or three miles away from where the bombers were aiming. The report confirmed that the middle classes were showing "the morale of the best Londoners. The main Bristol tension exists among the poorer working classes". It was not surprising.

Another group, who could not find permanent sanctuary in the rural West, did the next best thing: they abandoned the city by night. This nightly evacuation by the so-called trekkers reached huge proportions – it was estimated that when trekking was at its height, more than 10,000 Bristolians made their way out of the city as nightfall approached. The main roads out of Bristol witnessed a dusk convoy of cars and lorries crowded with people no

JF

longer prepared to suffer the experience of another air raid, and those who couldn't find any form of transport did the next best thing – they made parcels of food and blankets and walked out of the city. To where? To anywhere they could. Even a night sheltering under a hedge at the risk of catching a chill or worse was preferable to another blitz, they said. One observer described the evening scenes of departure as "like Picadilly in the rush hour".

It was good business for the farms, hamlets, villages and small towns within easy distance of Bristol. Rooms were snapped up by people prepared to pay well over the going rate for overnight accommodation. Village halls were commandeered by nightly evacuees who dossed down cheerfully despite the discomforts of this nomadic life. At least they were alive and at a safe distance from the bombs and from huddling in damp, cold, unreliable shelters near their homes. Some trekkers clubbed together and hired lorries to take them well away from the danger and to places where they felt doubly safe, like Burrington Combe with its cliffs and caves. Strange, gipsy-like communities sprang up in such places, resented by locals.

Those who stayed behind in Bristol to face the rigours of air raids were even more hostile to the trekkers – they jeered at them and derided them as the Yellow Convoy who slipped away to country funk-holes while others did their bit with fire-watching and fire-fighting, voluntary work and civil defence. The ones who suffered the most venom were the young and able who deserted

The violence of a heavy bomb's detonation sent this bus sprawling in Easton Road, Bristol.

JF

**Holy Trinity, Hotwells.
The destruction of
churches added to
the horrors of war.**

Bristol for country pubs in places like Saltford, Dundry and Long Ashton, spent
the evening at the bar and would only return at closing time if the sirens had
stayed silent. Otherwise they'd doss down at the inn . . . at a price, of course.

The authorities were angry and alarmed at this behaviour. A 'Stay Put'
campaign was launched, urging householders to stay by the properties and to
help prevent incendiaries spreading more fires and causing greater damage.
Various threats were made – that abandoned houses would be seized by the
authorities and used to rehouse the homeless from the blitzed inner city, that
ARP wardens would be officially sanctioned to break their way into deserted
homes and, unofficially, that fire-fighters wouldn't lift a finger to prevent a
trekker's home burning down if an incendiary happened to fall on it. The
trekkers listened to the arguments and threats, bore the criticisms and
jeers – and continued to vote with their feet.

Trekking, and evacuation, made a noticeable impact on Bristol's population.
One baker in Brislington, an area within easy walking distance of the
surrounding countryside and nearby villages and the town of Keynsham, said
that of 140 houses on his daily round, 50 were evacuated. A Bristol clergyman
reported that of 953 homes in his parish, 121 had been compulsorily evacuated,
80 voluntarily evacuated and 235 were empty at night.

One curious phenomenon seen in Bristol worried the morale-watchers. The
report said: "A striking feature in Bristol is the way in which people continue to

JF

inspect and gaze at damage with as much intensity as in other towns blitzed for the first time. This in itself tends to indicate a slow degree of recovery?" The question-mark left the matter hanging in mid-resolution. Veterans of the war on the Western Front of 25 years before could have diagnosed this morbid practice far more accurately. They could remember seeing similar behaviour displayed by shell-shocked troops among the ruins of France and Flanders, disorientated men who showed an obsessive fascination with scenes of destruction.

Bristol could only pray that the days of Easter would be held sacred by the Germans as the festival of Christmas had been. Their prayers were in vain. On Good Friday, as Christians recalled the Passion of Christ, the bombers returned. The sirens sounded at 9.46 p.m. and for the next two hours bombs fell from a cloudless night sky. Once again, there was a false All Clear signal to fuel people's bitterness and anger. The sirens sounded a new warning within 18 minutes and people fled back to their shelters as a fresh wave of bombers arrived to pile on yet more agony and destruction. The raid cost the lives of 180 people with 146 seriously hurt and another 236 slightly injured.

Just how shattered and bitter many people had become was made abundantly clear when the very symbol of Britain's pugnacious refusal to sue for peace, the Prime Minister Mr Winston Churchill, came to inspect bomb damage the day after the Good Friday raid.

The Bristol Museum suffered a direct hit . . . among the greatest losses was a magnificent collection of fossils of icthyosaurs and other prehistoric sea dragons.

Churchill touring wrecked Bedminster in the aftermath of a raid . . . he was booed by angry women who snatched away flags which had been given to children to wave in greeting for the Prime Minister.

Bill Graves:

'They brought Churchill down with some of the top officials of the Corporation and he went to various parts where bombing had taken place. They came to where I lived and they gathered up the school kids from the local schools like St Gabriel's and gave them flags and wavers to wave. There was such hostility from some of the women who lived near John Street where they'd lost friends and relatives that one of the women went and snatched things away. The police got quite upset about this. She was snatching flags and when Churchill actually turned up the women turned on him, became very hostile and started booing and shouting abuse at him.

Not only were they very tired, not only were they fed up with the bombing but they were also very, very hungry. There was a degree of malnutrition. Many people were living better as far as food was concerned than they'd been living before the war, but there were still people who couldn't afford to buy rations. With their already deteriorating health there was malnutrition, and that made people tired and irritable and this manifested itself on that occasion. People couldn't bottle it up any more and Churchill was the focal point. There was also a great deal of bad feeling against some of the officials. There were suggestions that there was a lot of black marketing going on. They were the epitome – they looked content. But look at us! We're down on our uppers! That's what came out at that demonstration. **'**

Movietone News, which had used pre-blitz film in its heavily censored report on the first great raid on the city, resorted to a fresh cover-up to disguise these unseemly scenes. The newsreel of the Churchill 'visit' showed cheering crowds and a grateful, plucky population ready and willing to take all that Hitler could throw at them. In fact, some of this uplifting footage had been filmed in Swansea. Such were the subterfuges to deny the truth of what was happening in Bristol.

Iris Caple:

'Children were upset, they were cold and miserable, getting no sleep. Parents' nerves were getting really ragged. It was night after night without an hour's sleep. Most people were just about fed up with it and they were saying that it was about time that it was all ended, that these wars should never be, that these wars were planned out by heads of state and the people left in the dark. A lot of the older people like my parents said they'd had enough. I think a lot of them were ready to give up. **'**

That mood of despondency had its echoes in most corners of Bristol as the last bombers droned away into the early morning sky on Saturday April 12, 1941.

Bill Morgan:

'I had had about two hours sleep all that week. That just gets you down. You think, I can't go on much longer and that was the feeling on that Saturday after the Good Friday raid. The human spirit can bear so much . . . there's a limit. Everybody was scared at heart. When you had this thing going on and on, all night and into the next morning, you dreaded what was going to happen the next evening and perhaps the next after that.

The general feeling I found by talking to people – and I thought the same myself – was that if there had been another raid on the Saturday evening after the Good Friday raid, panic would have arisen in Bristol. I think that would have finished us off in Bristol. The people had just about had enough. **'**

3. The struggle for survival

The West Country watched and waited for fresh hammer blows to fall on Bristol after the horrors of Good Friday. The citizens themselves counted the minutes and hours as evening fell on Easter Saturday and Easter Sunday, flinching at the prospect of further punishment. One more, just one more and tautened nerves would snap and chaos must surely follow. Something must be done. . . Bristol must survive. That determination grew and it would have grown with even more vigour if the city had known that the worst was now over. The Good Friday attack was to be the final full-scale blitz on Bristol.

It was time to look to the children who, with the women and the elderly, had been the main victims of the blitz, helpless and with none of the discipline and reassurance that war work offered to adults. Bristol's very survival depended on its future generations. Now Bristol must remove as many children as possible from the dangers of a city that seemed to be a prime target for the Luftwaffe.

When war broke out, Bristol had been categorised as a 'safe' city while London, 120 miles to the east along the Great West Road and the Paddington-Temple Meads railway had been considered decidedly unsafe, easy prey to enemy raiders. Even in the 1914-1918 war London had sustained air raids, from both zeppelins and from Gotha bombers while Bristol had escaped such attention. There was a mass exodus from London in the first days of World War II and much of it came West. Many thousands of Londoners passed through Bristol on their journey to safety and some of these decided to stop and stay in the area. When the great London blitzes began in earnest in September 1940, there was a fresh wave of refugees crowding into the West Country.

But the heavy raids on the Bristol area in November, December and January rapidly destroyed Bristol's reputation as a bolt-hole from the blitz, particularly since many of the settlers were staying in the more central areas where the bombs fell thickest. The raids themselves were of great intensity. Bomb for bomb, acre by acre, Bristol suffered some of the most concentrated air raids experienced in Britain throughout the war. Yet it was not until the worst was over that Bristol was officially classed as a dangerous place. That didn't come until May 1941. With the classification came funds and help, particularly in the form of billeting allowances and authorisation for the removal of women and children from the danger zones.

But if the bureaucrats who decided such matters were slow to act, the people themselves were not. The early stages of the war were marked by mass movements of people, particularly children. There was a steady stream of evacuations from town to country and many rural communities and country towns across the West of England became hosts to city children. The well-to-do were quick to ensure the safety of their families and those boarding schools which did happen to be in cities or in potentially hazardous areas near London or the South Coast were swiftly packed off to places which would be of no

Previous page: A mobile canteen bringing a little comfort to families made homeless by the bombing in Bath.

A nightmare world of chaos. Children walking through the ruins of Newfoundland Road in Bristol.

JF

interest to the Luftwaffe and which would be well away from the first wave of a German invasion. Clifton College was moved from Bristol to the peace of Bude in Cornwall while the preparatory school for Downside, Worth Priory, was evacuated from near Crawley, and uncomfortable proximity to much of the aerial action in the early part of the war, to the much safer environment of Downside's extensive grounds and buildings at Stratton-on-the-Fosse on the Mendips.

Several thousand children had left Bristol before the start of the blitzes and many thousands not only from Bristol but also London and other high-risk areas had been billeted on hosts in Gloucestershire, Somerset and other shire counties.

Many fled the Bristol blitzes that dreadful winter of 1940/41. They abandoned their homes in the city to live with relatives in the country or in

The refugee . . . an elderly victim of the Bath raids picks her way among the ruins.

JF

rented accommodation somewhere safe and quiet. Voluntary organisations like the Rotary Club and the Lord Mayor's War Services Council offered grants for the needy. While such volunteer efforts were badly co-ordinated and often haphazard, at least they helped some avoid the air raids.

As the raids worsened, the calls for Bristol to be granted the status of a danger zone became louder. A deputation of Bristol city councillors and other local leaders harried the Health Ministry on the need to remove as many schoolchildren as possible from a city where many schools had been damaged and some destroyed. Finally, on January 25, the Ministry accepted that Bristol deserved some special help. It was agreed that children living in south Bristol, Avonmouth and Shirehampton and what remained of the central areas could be evacuated with government approval and assistance.

Evacuation plans, spurred on by the constant threat of yet more attacks,

Homes gone but a doll's house survived and was rescued from the rubble of Newfoundland Road.

JF

swung into action. The first parties of elementary school children to be sent from their homes left Bristol for Devon and Cornwall in mid-February. More parties followed in April and May. Gerald Smith was one of those who left Bristol.

Gerald Smith:

❝The bombing became worse and it was decided the children should have the opportunity of being evacuated. My mother agreed that the three of us should go, my young brother, my sister and me. We were anxious because we didn't know where we were going. We thought we might even be going abroad. The ones to be evacuated were lined up in the school hall and then we were told to turn up with our kitbags the next morning. It was as quick as that. As we were lined up we were given labels and we hung them on our collars or shirts or coats

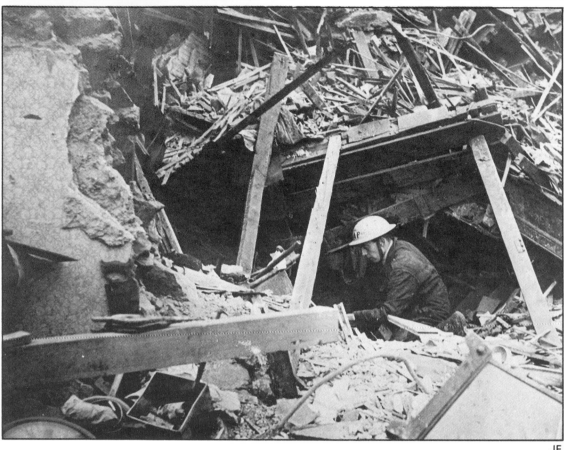

JF

A rescue worker trying to reach two women trapped under this bombed house in St Michael's Hill, Bristol.

and told we would be leaving the following morning. It came as quite a shock – we hadn't expected it to happen as quickly as that.

My parents were quite sad and upset but we were very, very pleased, war being a nasty thing and, I suppose, the tension of the war was beginning to tell on us. The next morning we lined up with our labels and our gas masks and the coaches were there. The parents started to cry. I couldn't understand why they cried because I thought they should be enjoying it like us. We all had sandwiches which disappeared before we got to Temple Meads station.

I had never been on a train and this added to the excitement. We pulled in at Weston-super-Mare and thought we were going to stay there but the train continued on and the journey took the best part of seven hours. Eventually we arrived at Bideford in Devon, very, very hungry and very, very tired. All the humour and fun had waned. We were herded into a hall and we were each given a bun and a hot drink. This gave us some pleasure and joy and then we went in double-decker buses to Clovelly. I didn't know where I was, I only found out later.

It was still daylight when we reached Clovelly and we saw the sea. But only the bottom deck was allowed off at Clovelly. We landed up at what I now know is Hartland in North Devon. We were herded into a hall – it was rather like a slave market. The bidders stood there and selected children. We noticed the crowd of children was diminishing, it was getting dark and then we were the

JF

only ones still stood around . . . my sister, my brother and me. Then it was dark and we were very, very sad. Nobody would have three children. We were pretty dirty at the end of all that day's travel and with all the dust and soot we must have looked a pretty sorry sight . . . a sniffy little boy of five, my sister and myself. They broke us up and my younger brother and sister went to a place five miles from Hartland. And then there was me. I was the last in the auction.

They walked me down a country lane to a house that was to be my home for the next 18 months. A policeman was there and when the lady came to the door, he said 'This is Master Gerald Smith and he's going to be your evacuee'. The lady looked at me with glaring eyes and said 'I'm not having that scruffy little bugger here'. I remember it so clearly . . . it was a tragedy for me. I went into a house where I felt very much unwanted. I looked out of the window in the moonlight to see the sea glimmering some miles away. I thought, Gosh, I've gone across to America! I didn't know where I was. They gave me a candle to go up to bed and I went to bed a very sorry and sad boy and cried the hours away.

But the next morning was a brilliantly sunny morning, I found myself in one of the most modern houses in the area and when I looked out of my bedroom window I found to my amazement that there were all fields and cows. I don't think I'd ever seen a cow close to before. I realised then that I was on a farm just like I'd read about at school, but here it was real with the dog, horses and cows. I could eventually milk a cow quite adequately and I became a very good

Jim Facey's handwritten caption on the back of the original photograph simply reads: "A resident of Stafford Street, Bedminster". Only the location needed to be recorded – the misery of total war was universal.

The chef of a wrecked snack bar set up his impromptu kitchen in the ruins of Mary-le-Port Street, one of Jim Facey's best morale-boosting pictures.

JF

farmhand, so the situation changed completely. My foster parents were the best I could have had – they turned up trumps. But that first night, I thought things were going to be dreadful. **'**

Back home in Bristol, with thousands of children now evacuated to safe places in the far South West and with a welcome lull in the bombing, the city began to clear up some of the worst bomb damage of recent months. Services were restored, shattered windows replaced and deserted homes made secure. Business as usual, which braver spirits had done their best to make the watchword during the grim winter of 1940/41, really began to mean something. Restoring some of the shattered fabric of the city went hand-in-hand with increasingly successful attempts to restore the shattered confidence of the bomb-weary people. More raids must be expected and the people must be

JF

given every assistance to help face fresh ordeals. The respite from raids worked its own, quiet change in morale, but more could be done. A change of scenery was bound to be beneficial and so it was that in the wake of the Good Friday raid, the Duke and Duchess of Beaufort offered the Lord Mayor of Bristol a site for a camp at Hinnegar on the Badminton estate in Gloucestershire. It is a delightful place, just off the road between Bristol and Tetbury and near the beautiful Worcester Lodge and the pretty village of Didmarton. It was just the setting to offer peace and calm to the war-weary.

Hinnegar was soon established as an important place of recuperation for young families. A temporary building acted as a dining room and recreation room and there were tents and camping equipment. News that the camp's facilities were available was passed around the city. Amy Granton heard about the camp when she went to her local baby clinic with her two-year-old daughter. It sounded like the tonic she so badly needed.

Amy Granton:

❝I heard they were sending people away for a holiday, the ones that had been through the bombing. So I applied for it. We'd been so tired with these blitzes and with raids nearly every night. We took a coach from the clinic to the camp at Hinnegar. First of all I didn't like it – I'd never slept under canvas before. To begin with they put me and my little daughter into this huge tent with big iron

A potent image of war. Nurses in a wrecked ward at the Homeopathic Hospital in Bristol.

JF

The post-raid efforts saw the mobilisation of every available hand to help clear up the mess. Here sailors work in ruined Bridge Street.

bedsteads, but then they moved us and we were in a little tent on our own. I enjoyed that.

There was a big hut where we had all our meals, and washrooms. There were probably about a hundred of us staying there. They had games for the children and the food was very good. You were all allocated jobs, to do the clearing up, to tidy your tent, to wash up. The worst job was washing the porridge pots – it was porridge and bread and jam for breakfast. But when that was done you were free, you could please yourself what you did with the children. We walked through the park with the deer and the quiet, the solitude of it all, it was so lovely.

In the evening they let us go into the village of Didmarton, as long as you got your child to sleep. Then helpers would keep an eye on them for you. We used to go to the pub in Didmarton and have a game of darts. There was a bomb disposal squad stationed there and they used to come in and play darts with us and generally have a laugh.

"The only thing I didn't like was the cows and invariably we had to walk through fields of cows. We used to sit around at night, outside our tents, when the children had gone to bed and we would all reminisce about what had happened to us in the war, about our husbands, about what we'd been through. And then we'd have a sing-song. It was really a proper jolly camp. Everyone was friendly – they'd all experienced the same things.❜

JF

Betty Screen has fond memories of the camp on the Badminton estate too. She was one of the many children who spent a fortnight there.

Betty Screen:

❝Mum needed a complete rest so my brothers and I were the three children taken with her. We were in tents and there were camp fires. I remember Mum, after putting us to bed, used to go out and have cups of tea with everyone else. They used to take it in turns singing or play-acting or somebody with a poem. Mum always sang Vera Lynn's 'White Cliffs of Dover' and we used to lie in our tents listening to her.

One night a cow came in the tent and started licking the blanket and I was screaming. It was dark and I thought it was some giant come through the door. The cow started backing out and all the mothers came running. Of course we all laughed when we realised what it really was. I think we laughed for hours.

Then we were out walking one day, lots of mums with their children, and one of my brothers was on about 'Whatever's this coming down the lane?' All we could see was a big piece of iron on tracks. As it got nearer and nearer we just stood there, mouths open, eyes wide open and then we jumped in the hedge. And it was a tank. It stopped right in front of us and the driver poked his head out of the top and told us not to be afraid.

We were told that Queen Mary was coming to the camp one day so the

Apprehensive Bristol children await evacuation from the city. For some, evacuation meant months of unhappiness, for others some of their best childhood memories in an idyllic countryside safe from the raids.

London evacuees arrive in the West Country. Bristol was declared a 'safe' area in the first year of the war and thousands of Londoners fled to the city.

mothers gave us all a bath and put our best clothes on. I was walking across a field and Queen Mary was coming from Badminton House across the grass towards a very long table with books spread out. Each child in turn was sent to her. My brother Roy and I held hands and walked towards her but my brother George wouldn't come. I thought she looked very stiff and regal. I thought she had rather a lot of make-up on, a lot more than I'd seen the women in the camp wearing. But when she spoke, it . . . she was so gentle, it was really nice. She bent down and caught hold of my hand and asked me what I thought of the camp, whether I was enjoying myself. She kissed me on the cheek and she turned round and took a book off the table and gave it to me. It was fantastic. I just couldn't take my eyes off her face. Then we were told to make our way into Badminton House where a room had been set aside for lemonade, cakes and games.

We had to sing a song which took us a while to learn. It goes like this:

'There's a gracious lady not far away
Brings sweets to our camp and kind things to say
When she visits the camp, it's red-letter day
For the camp of the Hinnegar Campers.'

The two week breaks at Hinnegar camp were just part of a much wider

campaign to provide holidays for those who had suffered in the air raids. A huge effort went into the exercise that summer, with families being offered free or almost free vacations in a bewilderingly wide choice of places. A large number of children were sent to Sand Bay and Brean Down near Weston-super-Mare. The people of Sidmouth in Devon offered billets to 100 Bristol families, at three days' notice and at no charge. Sherborne Girls School, empty for the summer holidays, took 150 Bristolians at a time for two week holidays and some Oxford colleges offered accommodation and peace among the dreaming spires.

Rural England looked lovely during the war, and its loveliness and serenity are a lasting memory to a generation who were young then. The war had taken away so many men from the farms that labour had to be concentrated on the essentials of producing as much food as cheaply and efficiently as possible. So, season after season, verges went uncut, hedges were untrimmed, woodlands were neglected and nature triumphed. Everywhere was growth and luxuriance with sparkling banks of wild flowers and country lanes edged with undergrowth and crowned by canopies of uncut hawthorn and hazel. Those who came to the country, as holidaymakers from the blitzed cities, as servicemen and women garrisoned in the West and as evacuees were enchanted. Pastoral England became forever associated with peace, calm and beauty after chaos. The contrast could not be greater – natural order against the artificial ruin and jagged skylines of the shattered city. The spell worked and, for many people, it

From city kids to country ploughboys . . . evacuation to farms was a lifetime's adventure for some.

Blitz-weary mothers and children in the peaceful surroundings of Hinnegar Camp on the Badminton Estate near Chipping Sodbury.

works to this day.

As Amy Granton remarked:

‘Being in the country did give me a great boost, so much so that I wanted to take a job there in the country after I'd been at Hinnegar. To this day I love the country, I love being in the country.’

Yet war could bring death and destruction to rural communities which had thought themselves immune from the raids witnessed in the cities. The pretty Cotswold town of Painswick, near Stroud, was astonished when it was attacked in the summer of 1941. Painswick had heard bombers often enough, but only because the town lay on the flight path to other areas. Black-out precautions were laxer than in the big cities. Peggy Perrin remembers the night of the attack vividly.

‘We used to have frequent sorties of bombers going over. We used to listen to them and think, that's Birmingham or that's Coventry. Then we'd turn over and go back to sleep. This particular night there had been a dance at the local hall and it was a hot June night. People had come home late, at about 1 o'clock in the morning. And there was a slight breeze blowing, people had their lights on and they said Painswick looked like a fairyland from the other side of the hill.

And there was a lone bomber, coming back from Birmingham or somewhere, and I think he thought Painswick must have been Brockworth, the aircraft factory in the next valley to us. He dropped his stick of bombs and that woke us up. We struggled out of bed and couldn't see a thing because every time anybody put a light on, air raid wardens were shouting to people to put out that

Hinnegar Camp. The two-week holidays gave exhausted, terrified mothers and children a badly needed break from the nightmare surroundings of the wrecked city.

so-and-so light.

Wilfred Pickles ran a radio series and he used to say, 'What would you do in a sticky situation? What would you grab first?' Well, I grabbed my fur coat, my wellies and the cash box and went rushing out into the street. The houses in our street were all made of pretty big blocks of Cotswold stone and all the stone had fallen into the road. It was like mountaineering over the stones until we got down to safety. We went to my husband's parents down the next street.

We came back the next morning to look at the devastation. There was a chap killed in the house next door to us and the owner's son was buried right down at the bottom of the bomb crater. Luckily he'd been sleeping in an iron bedstead and this had sort of collapsed and formed a tent over him. He was dug out alive – that was a bit of luck.

The air raid and the damage drew us all closer together. There were two people killed, both were evacuees from Eastbourne. Those that were homeless afterwards were soon found homes. The homeless were told, we can put you up, come and stay with us, that sort of thing. High and low sort of mixed in together.❞

The holidaymakers returned to Bristol refreshed, much of their spirit recovered. The absence of the bombers, increasing efforts to sort out the mess and disruptions the blitzes had left behind and a growing feeling of comradeship began to transform the mood. Bristol would be attacked many more times before the war was over, but it had survived one of the blackest chapters in its history. And then morale was given a further boost by news which transformed the whole outlook of the war and brought a sudden surge of optimism.

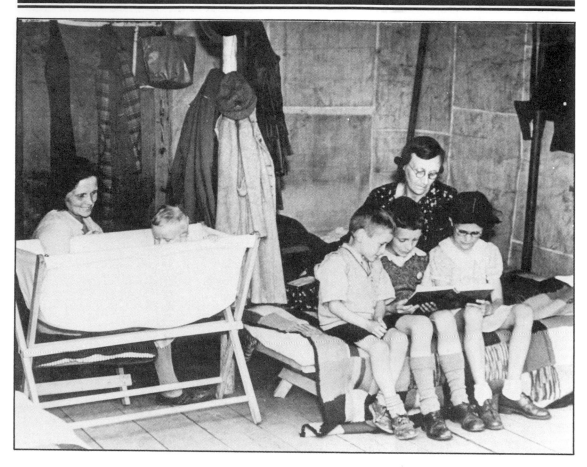

Story time at Hinnegar Camp. These holidays in the peaceful surroundings of rural England gave many town children a love of the countryside that has lasted throughout their lives.

In June it became blindingly clear why there had been the respite from bombing. On Sunday June 22 Hitler launched the greatest military force seen in history against the Soviet Union. The war's real purpose, the seizure of the great land masses to the east of Germany to create a vast German empire, was at last confirmed. The German bombers had done their job in the West, now they were needed on the eastern front. As the Luftwaffe bombers left, the Royal Air Force stepped up its own bombing operations over occupied Europe, even striking at Berlin itself. News that the Germans were now suffering what cities like Bristol had endured gave grim satisfaction. Britain now had a mighty ally in the Soviet Union and the tide of blitzes had turned back on Germany. Such news helped people face the hardships and shortages of everyday life.

The war at sea took its toll on the West Country, Britain's survival depending on importing food and other goods. London and the east coast ports were too vulnerable to attack so by 1940 the main west coast ports had become the chief naval gateways into Britain, via the Clyde, the Mersey and the Bristol Channel. The U-boat campaign, which had been adopted so successfully in the First World War, was stepped up and trade at both Bristol's City Docks and Avonmouth was severely reduced by the U-boat threat lurking out in the Atlantic.

Foreign corn was no longer shipped into Avonmouth in huge, pre-war quantities. The mills at Avonmouth were kept as busy as they could be under

Queen Mary meets refugees from the city at Hinnegar Camp.

the circumstances, but with home-grown, not imported corn. The banana boats, which had been such a well-known feature of the Bristol shipping scene, were no longer seen. The ships bringing animal feedstuffs no longer came. The boats bringing Irish cattle to Bristol stayed at home, afraid to venture into the Irish Sea. And those ships which did make the journey to Avonmouth or the City Docks found plenty of evidence of bomb damage, although none which had caused a great deal of disruption to the diminished trade. The City Docks had been hit the hardest, but the strategic importance of the ancient harbour was slight. The docks had been in decline for years. It was Avonmouth on which the nation relied so heavily and despite successive attempts to wreck the Severnside docks, the damage was slight. Some buildings had been lost and some wagons hit, but Avonmouth was never out of action. Its trade hit hard, certainly, but its wharves and cranes and labour force remained intact for the

The original caption to this posed picture taken in Avonmouth and approved by the censor on January 18, 1941 reads: 'The Flag still waves above damaged homes in the Bristol area. Whilst the owners searched for their valuables, they cheerfully exclaimed "The British flag will always fly"'. In reality, Bristol's morale was at breaking point.

huge efforts that lay ahead.

The drastic fall in imported food through Avonmouth and other British docks inevitably meant food shortages as well as shortages of clothing and other goods. Rationing had begun right at the start of the war and by 1941 shortages, queues for prized foods and other items and some new, unfamiliar fare had become a regular part of many people's lives.

Joyce Storey said:

‘Everything was rationed. We had about two ounces of bacon and a couple of eggs a week and everything was rationed down to about two ounces. Sweets as well; the older people used to save their sweets for the kiddies.

Every time we went out and saw a queue, we would join in. And when we got almost up to the head of the queue, we often used to say to people, 'What are we queueing for?' Everybody queued for everything. And a lot of things went under the counter and went on the black market. You could buy almost anything if you had the money for it.’

Iris Ford's family couldn't afford such extras and she discovered that wartime could bring some pretty strange food to family dinner tables.

‘I remember going to the market with my auntie and she said she was going to

queue for whale meat and try to get some tripe. She managed to get the whale meat in the end – there was a great long queue – but she got no tripe. She brought it home and we all thought this was going to be a great treat. But we took one bite of it and that was that. We all looked at one another and it all went straight into the pig bin where we put all the potato peelings and everything. The meat had a fishy sort of taste. It was similar in texture to meat but it had a very strong fishy taste, even with onions. You couldn't camouflage the taste. We didn't like it at all. **'**

A mobile shop comes to Bedminster. Despite the damage, life had to go on.

Amy Grant recalled that war-time food had some redeeming features as well as drawbacks.

' Well, you had the spam which was quite nice, really. I rather liked it. And you had dried eggs, which you could make into scrambled eggs and use in cakes. But meat was very scarce, of course. We could get sausages and you could queue for dripping at certain shops. But the sausages didn't cook well. You'd put them in a frying pan and they'd all go to bits because they were more bread than anything else.

I don't know what they made the dripping from, but my goodness, when you put it on the stove it used to make a horrible smell. We had margarine, not butter, and it wasn't like the margarine which you get today, which does taste nice.

Sugar didn't last very long if you liked your sugar, but I used to supplement my sugar ration with a tin of syrup when it was available and put a spoonful in my tea, which was rather nice. Children used to like it.

Fruit was scarce, of course, no bananas or oranges and when they were there, you had to queue for them too. We missed practically everything, but we just made do. If you gave up your jam ration, you could have extra sugar. I used to have lemon curd, which wasn't on ration, so much so that I detest the taste of it, even now.'

Food rationing varied month by month and was affected by how much was being imported from overseas at the time, but it settled down to an average weekly ration, per adult, of 2 oz of tea, 4 oz of butter or margarine, 2 oz of cooking fat, 8 oz jam, honey or marmalade, 8 oz of sugar, 2 oz of cheese, 4 oz of bacon or ham, 2½ pints of milk when it was rationed and a meat allowance of two small chops or half a pound of stewing steak. There was also a 'points' system for tinned goods like spam, baked beans and powdered egg.

Vegetables, bread, fruit, offal and fish were not rationed, but they were so rarely available that their non-ration status was almost meaningless. Away from the towns and cities, West Country families were well-versed in growing their own produce before the war began. Shortages – and the Dig For Victory campaign – made urban folk far more conscious of self-sufficiency. Flower beds became vegetable plots. Leftovers were treasured for chickens, rabbits and even pigs kept in town gardens. The movement was given impetus by allowing more and more open spaces to be dug up as allotments to eke out the meagre rations available.

The war became a period of make do and mend, of thrift and of often inspired recycling. And alongside this spirit of self-help came a new mood of co-operation as people 'swapped' and loaned to help friends and neighbours in need of some special item. Profligacy was frowned on – 'greedy pig' was a particularly damning phrase in war-time England – while skilful housekeeping in those difficult times became a national virtue. Drawers were filled with carefully folded brown paper and meticulously untied string for use on another occasion. There was hardly an item of household scrap that couldn't be turned into something to help the war effort along and children were encouraged to become collectors of useful scrap material like keys . . . to be melted down to make some vital piece of equipment for our soldiers, sailors and airmen, the campaigners said.

The clothes ration, introduced in 1941, forced Britons to become a nation of patchers, menders and re-users of old clothes. Hardly surprising at a time when, for example, the basic male ration was an overcoat every seven years, a pullover every five years, a pair of trousers and jacket every two years, a pair of pants every two years, a shirt every twenty months and a pair of shoes every eight months. Civilians soon began to look shabby, particularly compared with soldiers, sailors and airmen in uniforms, and new clothes were a rare luxury. But people did their best to keep up appearances with some very unlikely raw material, helped and encouraged by the large number of sewing classes which had been started.

Amy Granton:

'I managed to get hold of some barrage balloon material, which was silky. We made blouses and underclothes. It had seams in it, so you had to manipulate your way around the seams when you cut it. But my best achievement was with two grey army blankets. I made two coats and hats for both the children and when they went to Sunday School they had a march. I shall never forget it. I saw the children marching past my window with the coats I had just made for them.

From then on I used to experiment. I managed to get hold of a pair of officer's trousers with nice thin material. I made my youngest daughter a lovely coat, all pleated. She looked so bonny in that. I used to make their pyjamas out of any old discarded pyjamas and I used to knit for them and crochet too. **)**

People were determined not to allow the war to interfere with family celebrations, particularly weddings. Food might be short and new clothes near-impossible to come by, but everyone clubbed together to do their best to make these war-time parties go with a swing.

Bob Chappell:

(If someone was getting married, there was always the question of what and how you were going to get hold of things like bridesmaids' dresses and the bride's dress. Some people managed to borrow dresses from pre-war weddings of friends or relatives but it was more often than not that you knew someone that could get you a panel of parachute silk on the black market for fifteen bob and you could make beautiful bridesmaids' dresses and brides' dresses out of that. They used to dye the parachute material different colours, green, yellow and blue – that's how they got round that. **)**

Such domestic prudence and inventiveness in the face of severe shortages were reflected by the many public salvage campaigns, mostly run by the WVS. The WVS collected huge quantities of old clothes which were repaired and distributed and it ran sewing parties and the Housewives' Service to promote good neighbourliness. Everything that could be salvaged was . . . old pots, waste paper, old tramlines, kitchen waste, even old bones which, it was claimed, could be made into glue to help build more Spitfire fighters!

The international background had changed drastically. The Japanese and the Americans had joined the conflict after the Japanese attack on Pearl Harbour on December 7. It would be some time before the full impact of the American effort would be felt in the West Country, but the fact that we had another powerful ally as well as the Soviet Union made the hopelessness and the despair of that black winter of 1940/41 seem a long time ago.

The full force of the blitzes was over but air raids weren't, and Bristol remained a favourite target for the German bombers. The West Country was attacked on Saturday April 25 and Sunday April 26, 1942 and for a time it might have seemed that Bristol was in for a full-scale blitz. Knowle was particularly badly hit with 100 houses wrecked and another 1,300 damaged. But the Bristol raid was just the preliminary to the main event – the bombing of the historic city of Bath.

The Royal Air Force raids on German cities were becoming increasingly effective and causing severe damage to some of Europe's finest cities. Hitler was determined to have his revenge and so came the so-called Baedeker raids, named after the Baedeker guides to the main tourist attractions of Britain and the Continent. Bath, with its Roman and Georgian legacy, was selected as an obvious victim for this policy of tit-for-tat.

Bathonians had often watched Bristol blazing just a dozen or so miles down the River Avon and had heard the drone of enemy bombers in the night skies.

JF

The elegance of one of the world's most famous spas reduced to chaos. Emergency service workers rescue a sedan chair, symbol of a more civilised part of Bath's history.

But they had little direct experience of air raids, and certainly not large ones. Bristol was alert, prepared and ready for the enemy after its dreadful baptism of fire. Bath had no such experience to call on when the bombs began to fall.

Like most Bathonians, Joan Taylor did not suspect that the air raid sirens were a warning to her and her neighbours. Joan was engaged to a soldier and was living in Bath with her parents, brother and younger sister.

‘The sirens went but we didn't take a great deal of notice because they'd gone lots of times before and they were always for raids on Bristol. And it wasn't until my father and brother had actually gone to bed and I was getting ready to go to bed that I looked out of the landing window and saw that the crescent at the back of us was on fire. I called out the alarm in our big, old-fashioned house – we had the top flat – and we went down to join the people who were in the basement. We stayed there. They had two young children and there was my young sister. My brother had gone because he was in the Civil Defence. And we just stayed there and we could hear the bombs whistling down and then there was this terrible crash, a great thump and everything seemed to shake around us . . . and then there was silence.

Later we heard some men calling out . . . I don't know how long later. They were calling 'Is anybody there?' and they told us to come up and get out of the house as quickly as possible. When we came up the stairs from the basement

The mass funeral at Lansdown above Bath following the huge number of casualties during the Baedeker raid.

JF

into the hall, there were flames coming out of each doorway on the sides of the hall. As my mother was carrying my sister through the hall, the shawl around her caught fire. When we got outside into the street, somebody said, 'Go further up and get shelter wherever you can. The planes are coming down and machine-gunning us.'

The raiders returned the next evening and by then Joan and her family had been billeted in a school building. They spent the raid sheltering under the small, low school beds. On the morning of April 27, with the Baedeker raids on Bath at last over, Joan and her family made their way to the house where they had lived. It was a ruin.

‘We had no home left. All we had, more or less, were the clothes we stood in.

A mobile advice bureau at Bath. The war brought many unexpected problems which the Citizens Advice Bureaux did their best to solve.

The only thing that we did manage to save was mother's big tin trunk which we had had from the beginning of the war, one of those old-fashioned, heavy tin trunks. She had stored all the important documents and a doll that belonged to me and a few other things and it survived. It was found intact in all the rubble. **'**

The raid was even more cruel to Doreen Wall. Doreen was recently married and her husband had been sent overseas with the 8th Army in Egypt. In her husband's absence, she had been living in Bath with her parents.

'We had had quite a lot of bombing in the first raid and it was frightening. We were in the cupboard under the stairs. We didn't suffer anything in that first raid. The gas went and we had to light candles, a lot of soot came down the chimney and there was a lot of vibration.

But then they came back again to bomb Bath. I remember putting a coat on, because we were going to rush out and go into the street shelter, but we didn't have time to get out. The lady from next door came round to be with us, with her little boy, because her husband was out on fire-fighting duty at his firm. So we all crammed into the cupboard under the stairs. It was very frightening because it was so intense. They were dive-bombing a lot and machine-gunning. The noise was terrific. If you can hear bombs falling, whistling down, you know that that one's not for you. But when something hits you, you don't know

anything. The next thing I remember, I became conscious and I realised I was trapped. I couldn't move at all. Everything was dark. I did my best to move my head. I heard my Dad say something and I spoke to him and he told me to keep quiet.

Later on I heard the All Clear going and everything was all over me. I didn't think anybody would rescue us but they did in the end. We heard a lot of noise of clattering and calling. I was pulled out of the rubble. As I sat up on the stretcher, I looked around and saw this great big crater. Everything was filthy, including me. We were taken to some garages at the top of the road to wait for ambulances to take us to hospital and I remember the bumpy ride to the Royal United Hospital. Dad was in the ambulance with me and he was unconscious by then and very badly knocked about in the face. So was I, although I didn't realise it at the time. 』

They left behind two bodies in the shattered remains of the house. Both Doreen's mother and the small boy who had come with his mother to share their shelter died of their injuries. Doreen's father went on to spend eight months in hospital recovering from his wounds and Doreen herself underwent surgery for leg injuries with follow-up visits to specialists two or three times a week.

The Bath raids caused great confusion in the city. Bathonians had become

Trekkers leaving Bath. The war-weary of many cities like Bath and Bristol abandoned their homes during the danger hours of darkness and found shelter in the surrounding countryside wherever they could.

accustomed to the sounds and sights of Bristol under attack, but no-one had believed that Bath would become a victim of the enemy bombing campaign. Bath was ill-prepared. Bristol immediately lent a hand, sending across teams of Civil Defence workers who were by then blitz-tested and well experienced in coping with air raids and their aftermath. They were badly needed for the grim work that followed the attack. The bombs had killed 417 people and damaged thousands of houses. More than 200 historic buildings were lost.

The raids destroyed Bath's reputation as a safe place and there would always be that lingering doubt that the bombers might return one night. Nevertheless, despite the devastation and death, the injuries and the shock, morale remained good, possibly because of the short, sharp nature of the attack as against the repeated blows which had been aimed at Bristol. A cheerful propaganda film was made and was screened in cinemas across Britain. A more reliable examination of the mood of the city was made by Home Intelligence and that, too, confirmed resilience.

Another unexpected target was Weston-super-Mare. By June, 1942 Weston-super-Mare, like both Bath and Painswick, was used to the sound of enemy bombers in the night sky, but the drone had always meant trouble for others, not for Weston. Until the weekend of June 28 and 29, that is, when the peace that the coastal resort had enjoyed so far was suddenly and devastatingly destroyed. Babs Atherton was a warden on duty in the central area of the town when it happened. It was a clear, moonlit night and Weston had many holiday visitors staying, despite the war.

‘ In the early evening there were a lot of planes about but they seemed to be heading towards Bristol. And then all hell let loose. First came fire bombs and big flares which lit up everywhere and then the bombing began. When a bomb comes down, if you can hear it whistling, you know you're all right. But if it stops whistling, then you've got to hold your breath in case it comes a bit too close.

We were in the area around the Boulevard. There were an awful lot of fires at the High Street end of the shopping centre. My other warden and I had to patrol it whether there was a raid or not. We saw a plane come down off the hill, from the woods end, and we heard a bomb drop. We ran as the bomber dropped three in a line at Prospect Place. By the time we managed to get there, Prospect Place was just a pile of rubble and smoke, with everybody shouting. There were a great many people killed in Orchard Street, where they used to have the tall houses. It was Wakes Week from the Midlands so there were many people in the bed and breakfast places there. They never did know how many were killed there.

In Prospect Place there was a girl of about seventeen who was trapped under some beams. They tried all night to get her out. Dr Dennis Clark came with the First Aid team and crawled through the rubble to get to her with about six of us in a chain, passing things through this hole in the wall so that he could amputate her leg actually on the site. He had to. There was no other way of getting her out. They couldn't get anything through to her, they couldn't even give this girl a drink very well. Somebody brought along a little decorative teapot and they managed to get a drink to her using the little teapot.

The fires were so great that it became almost too hot to breath in the Boulevard area. The shops alongside the Boulevard were burning and a gas main exploded. There was a huge jet of blue flame but there was no time to deal with that. ’

The corner of High Street and the Boulevard in Weston-super-Mare . . . the raid killed many holidaymaking Midlanders as well as local people.

The fire watchers dealt with countless incendiaries that night and their work saved many buildings. Bristol lent a hand too. As had happened after the Bath raid, experienced Civil Defence teams from Bristol came hurrying across to Weston to help the resort's beleaguered and inexperienced crews. The bombers dropped about 47 tons of bombs on Weston, killing 102 and injuring a further 400. There was much damage to buildings and some familiar landmarks were wrecked beyond repair that night including the Tivoli cinema on the Boulevard and the town's main department store, Lance's in High Street.

These surprise raids caused a great deal of death and damage to the fabric of the towns which had been attacked but they did not weaken morale. Far from it. For almost two years the rest of the West Country had had to stand by as impotent observers of Bristol's terrible suffering. Now other towns had seen front line action too and the experience had strengthened their resolve and

Weston-super-Mare had prayed it would be spared the ordeal of a major blitz. The Luftwaffe thought otherwise and the destruction and number of casualties were considerable.

created ties of comradeship. There was a new, clearer identity of a nation at war. Babs Atherton remembers that spirit with pride and affection.

❛Everybody was looking out for everyone else. They were drawn together. It is something that doesn't happen very much these days, but then people would run in and out of other people's houses, there would be tea-making and you realised you needed one another to bolster each other up. It was a lovely kind of comradeship.❜

This spirit of comradeship and care for others did a great deal to alleviate the war's worst hardships and the inevitable post-raid reactions of depression and doubt. Tired, hungry people are easy prey to fears. Almost unspoken was the ghastly prospect of a life condemned to scratching a living in increasingly ruined cities until civilisation itself was destroyed by endless conflict – a nightmare which perfectly echoed the one which had haunted the front line troops in the trenches during the World War I who had believed that the war would never end. Such dark spirits needed exorcising . . . beyond them lay despair and defeat.

The way to counteract such morbid thoughts was with good news, optimism, looking on the bright side and relying on friends and neighbours. Ironically, those very people who had complained that the press and the censors had let

them down badly in their mealy-mouthed reporting of the blitzes in Bristol now began to accuse the press of reporting too much gloomy news. Newspapers and newsreels were urged, if not to dress up stories, at least to put them in a positive light. They were told to offer encouraging examples of gallantry, to stress small gains, not defeats.

And there was some good news. Britain's time as a nation alone was well and truly over, and Germany's relentless parade of victories had ground to a halt on the Eastern front. The United States had declared war on Japan and Germany following the attack on Pearl Harbour and the West Country's historic links with America and its strategically important maritime links between the Bristol Channel and the seaports of the East Coast became of great significance.

American aid to Bristol had begun at the very start of the war with gifts of money, food, clothing, medical stores, mobile canteens and kitchens and ambulances. American journalists had travelled to Bristol to report on the bomb damage and how the raids had affected the people. New Yorkers had tangible proof of the devastation caused by German bombers in the attacks on Bristol. Rubble from the blitz sites was transported across the Atlantic where it was used in the construction of the Manhattan section of East River Drive.

There is a plaque on the highway which reads:

❛Beneath this East River Drive of the city of New York lie stones, bricks and

A resort in ruins. The devastation around the Tivoli Cinema in Weston-super-Mare after the bombers struck.

rubble from the bombed city of Bristol in England . . . brought here in ballast from overseas, these fragments that once were homes shall testify while men love freedom to the resolution and fortitude of the people of Britain. They saw their homes struck down without warning . . . it was not their homes but their valor that kept them free. *

American entry into the war brought increased aid in food, goods and weapons. The Home Guard became better equipped. A quiet sense of confidence was growing. Gradually, some of those who had evacuated the cities began to think that it was time to return to their homes. The trickle grew to a steady stream of people. For children who had made a new life for themselves in the country like Gerald Smith, the re-adjustment to life in the city wasn't always an easy one. This was not the Bristol they had known and they explored its streets wide-eyed.

*The old Bristol had disappeared. Castle Street and all those well-known places around the Castle Street/Wine Street area had gone. The skating rink near the University had gone. The row of shops down Park Street was just twisted metal with iron girders knotted from the heat. *

But after a while the returnees become more accustomed to the bizarre landscape of a bombed city and the children found compensations. Some adults complained about the unruly behaviour of some boys, for with so many men called up and mothers tied to family or work, discipline was laxer than it had been in pre-war days. That gave children a chance to roam through a fascinating world.
Gerald Smith:

*We had to adapt to this new life in Bristol. We'd become used to the countryside, to playing in fields, to sunshine and cattle but we still had to humour ourselves and we found that there were still joys to be had. All over the city we found bomb damage and bomb craters. What craters could be used for swimming in, we used. And the bomb sites which could be used as playgrounds we used too. We always played soldiers. The game of Cowboys and Indians had ceased. We had our battles over the ruins and we fought the enemy and the enemy fought us and our joy and pleasure came from the ruins. We had many good moments there.
It wasn't all playing soldiers and playing battles. There were ordinary games like cricket and football and kick-around. We didn't have a football. It was a rolled-up piece of cloth which we kicked around on bomb sites which had been cleared of rubble. Of course there was no traffic either. We never had cricket balls either, so we'd make up a ball with old cloths and the great thing was that you could whack it, lose it in the ruins and immediately make up another cricket ball from blackout curtains tied with string. And that was our enjoyment. We soon came back to being city people once again, we became citizens of Bristol once more. But the country still rings in our hearts, for a lot of us. *

The return of the children and the sight of them turning the wretched piles of rubble and the empty bomb sites into playgrounds was a tonic in itself. Life must go on with its cycle of birth, marriage and death. A war-time marriage held great significance, all too often meaning painful partings and a very real dread that the couple might never meet again. But it was also an act of symbolic meaning in another, more optimistic sense. Shortly after the Weston-super-Mare raid, Babs Atherton was married in a war-time ceremony that was echoed in cities, towns and villages across the country: the younger generation pledging itself to a brighter, happier future. In Babs' case, the wedding was doubly poignant. It took place in the ruins of one of the churches which had been wrecked in the air raids.

‹I had a borrowed wedding dress and my bridesmaids had also borrowed dresses for the wedding. My mum did the reception herself, having collected a lot of bits and pieces from various relations. And I had a wedding cake. We all clubbed together – I had five sisters-in-law so I was lucky – and we got the cake made and took it to a baker and asked if he could ice it for us. We had managed to scrape together quite a bit of icing sugar but he said that unfortunately, because of regulations, he couldn't do us a white icing, that it would have to be chocolate. So we had a chocolate wedding cake.›

The struggle for survival was almost over. Make do and mend, comradeship, the war-time spirit and the changing fortunes of war had seen to that. Now the West Country would have even clearer proof that great nations were joining together to defeat the enemy. The Americans were coming.

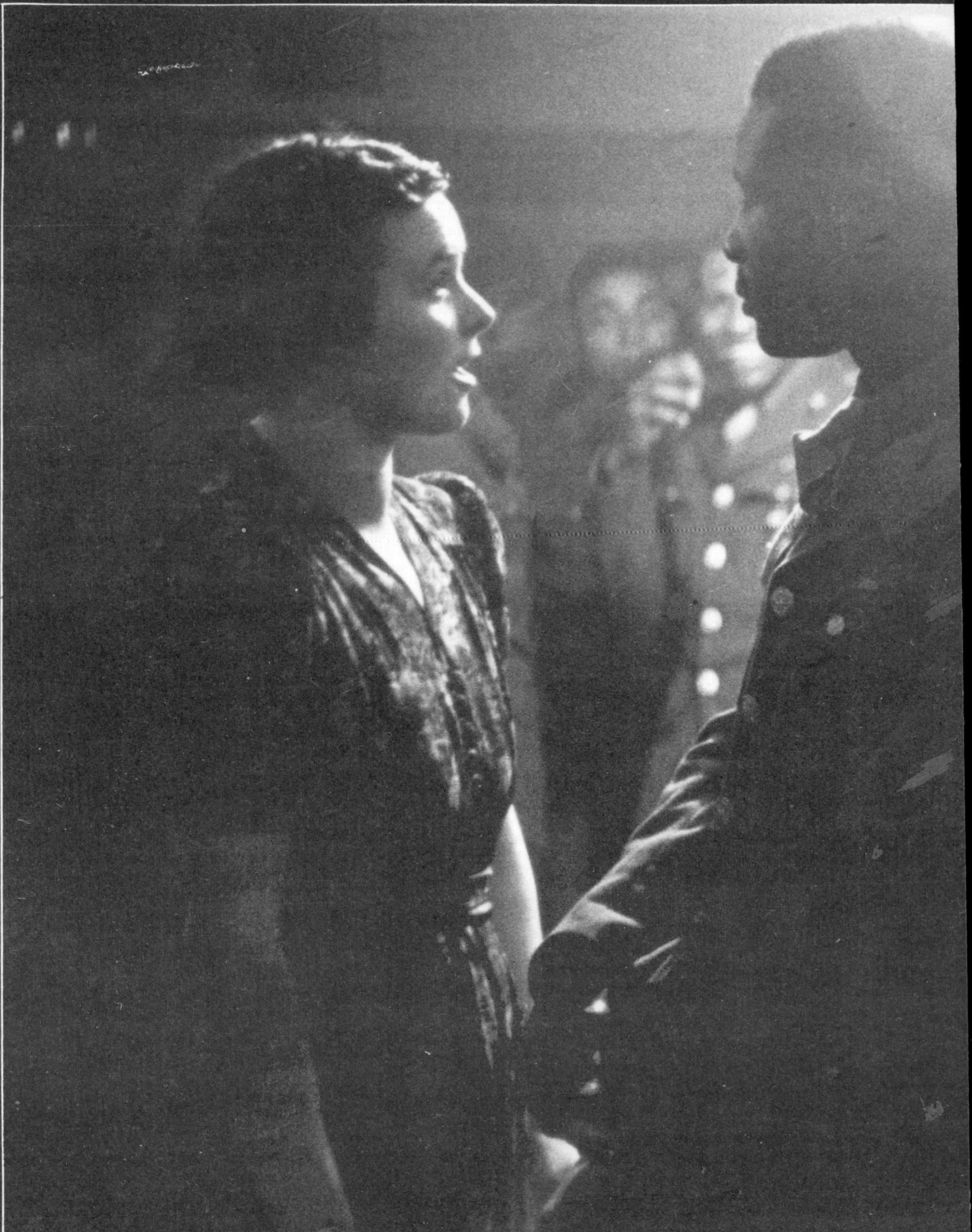

4. The road to victory

When the first American troops sailed into Avonmouth, in August 1942, they received a rapturous welcome, for everyone felt the war had entered a new phase. Britain no longer stood alone – the Americans, over-sexed and over-paid, were above all over here, and thousands of them now poured into the West Country, bringing with them gum and glamour, modern fighting equipment and a new hope of victory.

Bristol actress June Barrie, a child at the time, remembers the impact of the G.I's (so called because everything they wore was Government Issue).

'The Americans were billeted near us at the Greyhound Stadium at Knowle, and for us it was as if the cinema had come to life. They were so handsome and well groomed and clean, and the privates' uniforms were better than the ones our officers wore. And they were so generous, they used to leave food parcels on the wall for passers-by. The great thing for the girls was to go to College Green where the Americans would have jive sessions. I had a fat girl-friend who asked me to go with her. I was only 12 at the time and I knew my mother wouldn't approve, but I sneaked out of the house. We got some lipstick and tried to make ourselves look older, and we went to College Green. We found two suitably short Americans who were very nice to us, treated us absolutely seriously, though we were only little girls. They took us to a café in Cheltenham Road and bought us a mixed grill and then put us on the bus home.'

Iris Ford dated an American soldier.

'The date was fixed up by my brother who was about seven then. 'You be at the top of the road at 2.30 to meet an American called Jim' he said. I didn't believe him, but when the time came, I looked out of the window and there he was, very nice, very smart. So I went outside and said Hello. That's how our relationship started. We used to go to the camp dances to jitterbug, we won a competition once, and the prize was cartons of Lucky Strike. We went to dances all over Bristol, to the Victoria Rooms and the Royal West of England Academy, which was turned into the American Red Cross; they used to serve coffee and doughnuts. There was a lovely atmosphere at the dances, we'd do the jitterbug, catching hold of one another's hands and gradually being twisted round, swung under their legs and then over their heads, it was quite energetic. But we were young, we could manage it. We also used to do ballroom dancing to the big band and Glenn Miller records.

The Americans were so much better off than our boys – they got about £43 a month, while our men only got a few shillings. But the Yanks were generous, always buying us treats and saying nice things to us, they treated us like duchesses. Yes, some of them were only out for what they could get, but most of them treated us with respect. They weren't all sex mad. The local boys resented

Previous page: A black GI asks a white girl for a dance. The unprejudiced attitude of the British caused much racial tension between black and white American troops in Bristol and elsewhere.

them – they used to call girls who went out with Yanks 'spambashers' implying we went out with them to get presents of food. But a lot of romances developed, and I got very fond of Jim, and the subject of marriage came up. My father said 'no, you're too young, I'm not letting you go over there.' Jim was only 19 and I was only 15, and after that we had a difference of opinion and I didn't see him again until he left for D-Day. He came round at half past two in the morning, saying the camp was moving out. We sort of kissed goodbye, and he went. **'**

American troops watch a cricket match on the Close, Clifton College, where part of the D-Day operation was planned.

The G.I's were exciting, the girls said, and they smelled so nice. They used deodorants and aftershave, something British men did not, and they had a special charm; they treated girls like ladies. Madge Read was bowled over.

'They were fun, something new, when life was pretty mundane and most of our fellows were away. We thought of the American boys as Hollywood stars, we knew nothing about the awful race problems or anything like that. We always met them by going to dances, there were regular tea-dances at the Berkeley in Queen's Road, and there were always Americans there because they had a canteen nearby. The neighbours didn't always approve because after a dance finished at midnight, the Yanks would bring us home in their trucks, and I can remember neighbours banging on the windows and saying 'get to bed'. My father sometimes gave me a belt for being late home. **'**

For a lot of girls, the Americans were their introduction to sex.
Madge Read:

‘I was too young at the time, but I don't think they took advantage more than
any fellow would have taken. Maybe they were a bit fresh, but if you are
thousands of miles from home and the girls were after you, you'd take what you
could get, wouldn't you?’

Some of the relationships did turn out to be permanent, and at the end of the
war dozens of West girls sailed away to become GI brides, or married in Bristol,
like Iris Gillard's sister.

‘When they were engaged we used to get wonderful food parcels from his
family, and clothes and sweets and magazines. When they got married in
Bristol, they sent material to make the wedding dress and two bridesmaids'
dresses, it was out of this world to get such beautiful fabric when we were
making our underwear out of parachute silk. My mother made the dresses and
laid them out on the bed ready for the next day, and that night there was a raid,
and our windows were broken and the dresses were covered in broken glass.’

But of course the Yanks were not just over here for fun. The object of the GI
'invasion' was the preparation for D-Day and the South West was the gateway
for that final push, though this was all kept highly secret.
    The nerve centre for D-Day plans was Clifton College, where General Omar
Bradley set up his headquarters in the hallowed buildings, symbolically
watched over by the statue of Earl Marshal Haig, hero, and some said villain of
World War I. In the school's council chamber, Bradley prepared Operation
Overlord, while officers chewed gum in the classroom and played baseball in
the Close.
    The rest of Bristol was crammed with Yanks; there were camps at
Bedminster, Knowle, on Shirehampton golf course, at Westbury-on-Trym,
the black soldiers were based at Muller's Orphanage, and a hospital, later given
to the city, was built at Frenchay. The officers were billeted in private homes.
An airstrip was built in Ashton Park so that VIP's could come and go in secrecy.
    Somerset too was full to overflowing. An American headquarters was set up
at Taunton (where Musgrove Park became another hospital gift) and divisions
were stationed all over the county; six hundred black troops were sent to
Montacute where they were a great novelty, and a vast depot was built at
Norton Fitzwarren, as well as an immense petrol store at Highbridge.
Gloucestershire, too, became home to countless Americans, and thousands of
medical staff were billeted near Dursley.
    The effect on the local population was dramatic. Suddenly all the towns were
full of Americans, buying everything in sight. They filled the pubs, dubiously
drinking the warm weak English beer, they ate the fish and chip shops empty,
filled all the cinema seats and of course monopolised the local girls. But few
grumbled, because they believed the end of the war was in sight, now that the
Americans had joined them.
    When the Yanks had arrived in the West, in 1942, the weary population
might have been forgiven for thinking that the worst of the raids was now over.
    But one more major incident in Bristol, more terrible in its horror than any of
the others, was to come. On August 28, 1942, in Broad Weir, three buses were
blown up when a single raider, high in the sky, and so undetected, delivered

A rare picture of a black GI, who joined these Muller orphans at the Bristol Zoo. The black troops were billeted at the Muller Homes on Ashley Down.

death in the form of a 500 lb. high explosive bomb. In this massacre, 45 people died, most of them women and children, and 56 were injured.

No siren went, no anti-aircraft guns fired, until after the bomb had fallen and rescue services and fire engines were delayed by rush hour traffic. The loss of life was extra high because Broad Weir was being used as a temporary bus terminus – the usual terminus had been damaged. In fact the buses were not bombed: they caught fire from the petrol and burning fragments from a private car which received a direct hit.

Yet miraculously, a few did survive the inferno. Margaret Lowry was upstairs on one of the buses.

‛We were just moving off and I was looking out of the window when there was this almighty flash – we didn't hear the bomb because it was too close. Then the blast came, but the bus went on. I was told later that the driver had been killed instantly and that his foot was still on the pedal. The blast was like an iron hand in a velvet glove, it kind of tightened you so you thought you were going to burst and then let go, and came back again. After it had passed, I looked at the girl I was with and she wasn't there. I couldn't see very well, it was all dark. I felt the seat and she wasn't there so I got down on the floor and felt around and she wasn't there, and I found someone's head without a body . . . it was getting hot, the bus had caught fire.

❛There was a man sitting there and I said come on, and he didn't move, I touched him and he kind of collapsed, so I felt my way to the back of the bus and I found my friend just standing there, looking dreamily into space. I said we've got to get off, and she said yes, we've got to find a hospital to help all these people. And we got off the bus, I don't remember how, maybe we jumped down the stairs, and we ran off in the wrong direction to the hospital. I collapsed by a garage and they came out and took us in there and tried to bandage the wounds. There weren't enough ambulances so I had to go up to the hospital in the back of a baker's van. I'm tall and my feet were hanging out of the back all the way. I thought I was dying, I was quite sure of that. I was cut by shrapnel and glass and my face was all bloody. I remember putting my hand on a white board at the hospital and seeing a bloody handprint. I was bleeding so much that the blood prevented me being burned. I was very lucky.❜

Ken Simmonds was also at the scene of carnage. He worked at a nearby factory and ran out when the bomb fell.

❛We all rushed round the corner and saw the three buses, and a gang of us made for one in the middle of the road and started pulling people out as fast as we could. Then the bus caught fire and it started working back to us so we could not stay there very long. Most people were unconcious or dead, one or two were screaming but the trouble was we couldn't get at them, because the bodies were all on top of one another, legs were trapped and the seats were blown over and you had to kind of unravel people to get them out. Then the fire brigade arrived and the ambulances and as I was a part-time fireman I gave a hand and got a hose pipe onto the flames.

I saw some terrible sights, one chap had his head chopped off at the scalp. I went around later helping a man count the dead bodies, and in one of the buses I saw the driver, and he'd been killed by the blast and then the fire had made his body swell up like a rice pudding. A dreadful way to describe it but that's what it was like. The memory of that day is rooted in my mind, especially of the man who was concious and crying 'For God's sake get me out', and we couldn't get at him because of the flames. That evening I went out for a meal and I just couldn't eat it. I took my girlfriend to the pub and although I'm a teetotaller, that night I bought a pint, to try to make myself sick, to get the horror out of my system.❜

(A similar horror had occurred at a Gloucester bus terminus on Easter Sunday that year; 30 were killed and 159 injured when a bomb fell beside some buses loaded with passengers)

The Broad Weir bombing cast a pall of gloom over Bristol at a time when, worldwide, there were setbacks in the Allies' advance. The American

involvement had not brought the immediate victories everyone had expected. Montgomery had triumphed at Alamein, but the Japanese advance in the Far East was making massive demands on manpower and munitions. The warworkers of the West were called on to work even harder than ever and fresh calls went out for more women to work, even those with children.

For conscription had come in for women, from December 1941. As well as working on the home front, coping with queues and rationing and make do and mend, women who were single, or whose husbands were not at home, were expected to join the services or the civil service, or do war work, if they were between the ages of 19 and 51. Only women with children under the age of 14 or those caring for evacuees were exempt and now they too were asked to volunteer, and creches were set up.

There seemed to be no job which women could not do; they drove tractors, they made bombs, they built aircraft, they drove buses, flew barrage balloons – and the experience changed them for good.

Joyce Storey was one of the mothers who answered the call.

❛The war swept away a lot of mid-Victorian pre-conceived ideas about the roles of men and women. For us it opened up new horizons, and by acquiring new skills we found we could do things we never thought we were capable of doing. We found a new independence and a new self-esteem, we had money in

Women were conscripted into the munitions factories; a woman confidently takes charge of a load of high explosive bombs.

our pockets, we could do what we liked. '

Joyce Storey had a small baby but this didn't deter her from working.

' The war couldn't stop because you had a baby, my sister looked after her, so it was no problem. I worked with two large milling machines. As one stopped the other started, and there was a large circular saw that cut slots in a cylindrical piece of metal. An inspector would come round with a micrometer several times during the night to make sure all the slots were the same length. It was very repetitive and boring and all you wanted to do was sleep, often I would fall asleep on the bus home and go way past my stop. '

Irene Crew worked on torpedoes, and still suffers from the after-effects.

' To get to the job I had to walk about a mile before I started, and that meant climbing over an old railway place and going through tunnels, because it was a secret factory site, well hidden away. I worked there seven days a week on 12 hour shifts and I ended up with arthritis. '

As a complete contrast, May Rae took a job on the Bristol buses. Women had never worked for Bristol Tramways except in the World War I, as clippies, and when the men came home there were riots because the women had taken their jobs. But in the second war, no-one objected to women taking over. May Rae worked first as a conductor and then as a driver.

' I was conducting on the night of the terrible November raid, on the Sunday. We were going into town from Brislington and when the siren went we dropped the passengers at the nearest shelter, that was the regulation. The driver had to take the bus back to the depot while I went to Old Market Street to pay in the money. I was in the underground canteen when the bombs started and the police brought children in from the Empire Theatre nearby, and we played tunes to them on comb and paper. When we came out, we walked up West Street and I could see people in doorways. I thought they had fainted and wanted to help, but in fact they were dead from the blast. '

May had to cope with fights, because the buses were always so overcrowded.

' I used to say 'why don't you settle it outside', and get them off the bus. There were always queues for the buses, at any time of the day and we really packed them in, not like today. Then I applied to become a driver. I think 80 applied and only 22 passed and I was one of them. We had a month's tuition, which was a bit heartbreaking at the time, they were so very strict. It was hard work driving in the dark, because you couldn't see where the bus stood. In one road there was an avenue of trees and they painted white bands on them so we could count to the bus stops. One night I left an inspector behind, I just couldn't see him in the dark. The bus headlights had masks on them and inside all the lights were shielded and dim, so the conductor couldn't see without a torch which they had fitted on their bags. One time at a road junction, I was stationary and the bus was swiped by an American lorry driven by a soldier's girlfriend and another time I was coming down Park Street and the servo brakes, which you had to pump, failed, and I hit a van in front. Those were the only accidents I had. I liked the job, people were so friendly, we women drivers really felt we were the cat's whiskers. **9**

Few women were armed to fight in the front line, as Babs Atherton was, working as an ARP warden in Weston-super-Mare. She helped rescue the injured in the Baedeker raid there in 1942, and during the invasion scare was taught by an RAF sergeant to use a rifle.

6 It was suggested that young women might like to do something to help in case of invasion and a group of us at the library where I worked volunteered to learn to use a rifle and a revolver. We had instruction once a week and we'd practise; it didn't half give you a bruise on the shoulder, from the kick-back. I don't honestly think that had it come to the push I would have killed anyone with a rifle, but you never know: if it was your nearest and dearest, you might be brave enough. **9**

Another difficult and dangerous job that women did was to fly the mighty barrage balloons. At first this was considered men's work, but later in the war teams of WAAFs learned to launch and control these silver monsters on the end of flexible steel cables. The barrages at Avonmouth, Shirehampton and the Downs, and at several sites in Somerset were all run by women, who had to be on duty all round the clock, manoeuvring the balloons according to wind and weather and letting them fly higher when enemy planes were on the way.

Students were not exempt from war work either. Joan Collins was due to start at Bristol University when war broke out.

6 To avoid being called up, students had to produce a signed statement that you had spent 48 hours a month each term, doing voluntary work, and your record was assessed every six months. You had to do regular fire-watching as well. If there was a raid we were under the local branch of the NFS; one night a grocery warehouse got hit and thousands of tons of sugar and jam went up in flames. The smell of hot jam always brings that night back in the same way that Dvorak's *New World Symphony* brings back the night in the Colston Hall, when most of Park Street went up in flames. The hall was cleared and a gang of students, including me, volunteered to fight the fire, and we all yelled defiance in the rhythm of the New World theme – pom pom pompom, pom de deedle pom. Often we had jobs that were particularly dreary: I worked for a time in a small munitions factory and in a hospital kitchen where I shall never forget washing the mince under the hot tap, before cooking it for the 'gastrics'. **9**

Joan was injured during the Bristol blitz when an unexploded bomb blew up in one of the university buildings. By the time the war had ended, she had been a clerk, a farm labourer, a schools broadcaster and an aide to the Bristol Information Officer – and she got her degree as well, at a university which was packed to the roof with students because Kings College London had been evacuated there.

The aircraft factories, all-male pre-war, filled up with women workers. Kathleen Pursey went to Gloucester.

6 I worked on the undercarriage doors of the Lancaster bomber. I set hinge beams, I cut them on a jig and drilled them, I countersunk them, I put the Simmonds nuts on with rivets. It was very interesting after the shirt-making job I'd had before, and it was piece work, you could make good money sometimes. At first we didn't have a radio in the factory, only a gramophone, but then we got one and listened to 'Music While You Work', and we'd be hammering and drilling away quite happy, they could have gone on playing for hours as far as I was concerned. But in April 1945 we women were called to the office and told our work was finished, and I was told I would have to go back to shirt-making. I didn't want to go back, it was so boring after doing aircraft work, but that's what I ended up doing: making demob shirts. **'**

Another way women kept up morale was through entertainment. Actress Peggy Ann Wood kept the Little Theatre's Rapier Players going all through the war, while her husband actor Ronnie Russell worked as a special constable. She mounted 250 productions, and the only time the theatre was closed was for a fortnight at the outbreak of war and for a few months while the company went on an ENSA tour. Isabell Shaddick joined the Bristol Wartime Entertainers, playing the piano in factories and canteens and leading community singing.

'We used to go sometimes to the Wills factory in Bedminster and give a dinner time show for the workers. They enjoyed it, especially the community singing. They liked 'If You Were The Only Girl In The World', 'We'll Meet Again', 'Roses of Picardy', things like that. I think it gave them a boost to go back to work. Mostly we did shows for the troops, it was all voluntary work, but the government allowed us petrol so we could drive to the army camps. We used to go as far as Salisbury Plain, where once we saw some doodle bugs going over. The American troops would send jeeps for us and we'd perform and after the show we'd be invited into the officers' or sergeants' mess for a drink. And then of course I had to go to work in the morning. **'**

All-girl bands were another wartime feature: one of them, fancifully named Love Harris and Her Sunbeams, played at the troops' canteen in St. George's Road, Bristol, to the delight of the Americans.

Another mighty army of women workers was the WVS, who were everywhere in their green uniforms, providing tea and snacks to the firefighters and rescue squads, helping bombed-out families, collecting and supplying second hand clothes, collecting scrap, organising billeting, and driving mobile canteens. In Somerset, the WVS 'adopted' Lambeth in London, and collected furniture and household equipment for people whose homes had been destroyed, and some of them went to London to relieve the pressure on housewives, who came to their Somerset homes for a rest. In Bristol the WVS received the Dunkirk troops, fed and clothed them, trained drivers for ambulances and of course made million upon million cups of tea, even when the weather was so bitter that the tea froze in the cups.

The war work seemed endless, to men and women alike, but by the end of 1942, there were important victories in the Middle East and spirits began to lift. The turning point of the war seemed to have arrived and everyone celebrated in the West factories, and repeated 'War Weapons Weeks' and 'Wings For Victory Weeks', with processions and appeals for money to help the war effort. These events raised astonishing sums: small towns like Dursley and Thornbury regularly raised over a quarter of a million pounds.

The last of the major raids was over. With Hitler occupied on other fronts, there were no raids in 1943, and only 38 high explosive bombs fell on Somerset despite the fact that it was an area of ever-increasing allied air activity.

But Bristol was to suffer one last raid, on May 15, 1944. Avonmouth, crammed with equipment stored in readiness for D-Day, was attacked, with one casualty, and more bombs fell on Bedminster Down, where Tess Broughton was living.

❛My daughter Pauline had been evacuated but she had been back for a fortnight, and in the middle of the night I heard a plane going over and I said 'that's a German plane.' She said 'there's no more German planes, you've got them on the brain' but then the guns started up and the pilot dropped his bomb load in the valley at Headley Park and of course blew our bungalow sky high. I had kicked my mother-in-law and daughter into the shelter, still arguing that it wasn't a German plane and if I hadn't, they would have been killed. No-one in Bristol at the time realised we had been bombed out and I had an awful job persuading the authorities to get my husband home, no-one would believe it. They said the bombs were finished. I was furious, I thought that we were getting back to normal life. We were put in a house in Mansfield Street, Bedminster, it had been empty for 25 years, and when a reporter came to see us the next day, he told us it was haunted! The house just had bare boards and we had nothing, no clothes, we lost everything.❜

The green-uniformed WVS workers were always there in a crisis, handing out tea and sympathy. During the raids, many of them were wounded and 214 were killed.

For this last raid, the Germans claimed that "Bristol was attacked by a strong

The ten mile square
underground quarry
that became an
ammunitions dump for
D-Day.

formation of heavy bombers and the attack was a very sharp one and a great quantity of incendiaries and heavy explosives were dropped.'' At seven minutes past three on the morning of May 16, 1944, the All Clear sounded for the very last time, and the German bombers headed for home and never came back. Bristol and the West's ordeal was over, and three weeks later came D-Day.

The preparations brought a frenzy of activity in the region, which became one vast arsenal. Eric Banham remembers:

‘Beneath the village of Monkton Farleigh in Somerset there is a vast stone quarry, about ten miles square, and from 1943, it was an ammunition store. Around 17,000 men worked there and it was all highly secret. Before D-Day there was 12 million tons stored there, the equivalent of the atomic bomb that was dropped on Hiroshima. If it had blown up there would have been a crater

and a lake that stretched for 30 miles or more. Before D-Day the place really filled up; the amunition came in from the factories by rail, it was checked and tested and issued, and as fast as one lot came out, another lot went in. There was an immense flotilla of army and civilian lorries taking the ammunition to the coast area and work went on round the clock. ❭

The underground quarry at Monkton Farleigh became a factory cum arsenal in the build-up to D-Day.

The actual secret of D-Day had been well kept: though everyone knew the invasion was coming, no-one knew where or when it would take place. In the last days of May and the first days of June, the West knew something was up, as troops returned to barracks, and the roads filled up with convoys of vehicles and tanks. The Portway in Bristol, and Ashton Park, became parks for tanks and aeroplanes, and at Avonmouth Docks every possible space was used, right down to a butcher's cold store, which hid landing craft. Ten firms in Bristol sent the parts of Mulberry Harbour, which they had been making in secret, to the docks; it had been designed by the Admiralty in Bath and named after the tree at Kingsdown School.

At least one Bristolian knew the secret of D-Day well before everyone else. Edward Bracey was designing a new bakery for the Co-Op in Brislington when he was summoned to the War Office. There General Eisenhower told him that they wanted to hide invasion secrets in his ovens. Mr. Bracey built his new bakery, and stored maps, plans, French money and detailed instructions for the invasion there, until June 6, when he was able to bake his first batch of bread.

In Somerset ammunition dumps began to appear by the roadside, and strange vehicles, rescue launches, landing barges, steam tugs and amphibious vehicles were seen going down country lanes; every bridge in the county had to be measured to make sure that no precious equipment got stuck. On the

Munitions arriving by rail at Monkton Farleigh.

airfields, strings of gliders appeared and by May 31, embarkation began, and the troops and their massive supplies moved into Devon and Cornwall. The game was afoot, and suddenly the Americans had gone. As the *Western Daily Press* said: "The young men came, they conquered and they are gone – literally vanished overnight."

When the success of the D-Day landings was announced on the news and in the press there was great relief and rejoicing, mingled with worry about the fate of the Americans who had become friends of the local population. But then fell another shadow: the doodlebugs had arrived.

This new and almost surreal weapon, a pilotless robot plane, a flying bomb, had been launched on London with devastating effect and the West was wondering when their turn would come. Bill Graves was working on the railway at the time.

‘We were travelling to places like London and Bedford, which had been hit by doodlebugs and we heard talk of the V2 rockets from other railwaymen. People were saying it would be back to the blitz again and folks started leaving London and coming to the West again. They told us how frightening the new weapons were, how you didn't hear anything except the explosion. How could Purdown Percy, the local big gun, blast away at something like that?’

Gerald Smith:

‘At first we thought that the doodlebugs and V2's could never reach Bristol but then they extended the range and we wondered when it would be our turn. Every door slammed, every aircraft you heard, you thought it was a

doodlebug and you looked for a place to run to. **9**

Part of the vast underground munitions dump at Monkton Farleigh.

In fact none reached the West . . . but only because the D-Day advance prevented it. Rocket launchers aimed at Bristol were captured by the invading troops, just in time.

And progress after D-Day was not as fast as had been hoped. There were depressing set-backs, especially at Arnhem, and the advance to Berlin was slow. At home, there were increasing problems caused by the racial segregation policies of the American army.

The separation of men into black and white fighting units, housed in separate camps, and with separate entertainment facilities, came as a shock to the British and they did not want to play it by American rules.

Officialdom found it hard to know how to react: Sir Hugh Elles, the Regional Commissioner, asked the War Office for guidance. But a Worle vicar's wife had no doubts. She told her husband's parishioners that if a local woman kept a shop and a coloured soldier entered, she must serve him "but must do it as quickly as possible and indicate that she does not wish him to come there again." "If a woman is in a cinema, and she notices a coloured soldier next to her, she should move to another seat immediately." But the majority of West Country people were not as prejudiced.

They found the white Americans' attitude to the black troops offensive. Bill Graves remembers:

6 Bristol had always been easy-going about blacks, we'd had black people in the city for years and years because of the docks, and they were accepted. When Bristolians saw the brutality with which the black troops were treated by the military police, the way they piled into them with their truncheons, well it left a nasty taste, and they became more sympathetic to the black Americans than to the white. **'**

Mostly the cause of the trouble was that white girls would go out with black soldiers. They liked their beautiful manners and they were excellent dancers. The white Americans resented this bitterly, not understanding that British girls knew nothing of American segregation laws. It also appears that the white Americans in Bristol were mainly from the South, and so deeply racist.
Bill Graves came across evidence of this.

' There were many incidents of white G.I's going down to the 'black' pubs like the Spread Eagle in Old Market Street, and starting a fight if they found white girls there. Once there was a group of white paratroopers who literally hunted in packs, looking for black men to beat up and it turned into a riot. I was with two friends and we stood in the cinema doorway in Old Market and watched it happen, as they fought along Old Market and into West Street. Everyone says it didn't happen and no records exist, but it did, it was hushed up. **'**

Iris Gillard also remembers the same incident.

' My father was firewatching that night, and he cycled through the riot as it reached Trinity Church. He said the soldiers were using their bayonets and one man got stabbed. That fight went on for a night and a day and nothing official was ever said about it. **'**

But the authorities could not cover up a major battle in Bristol on July 15, 1944. Trouble had been simmering all that week because the blacks felt the way the recreation areas of the city had been carved up was unfair, giving them the use of the city's least desirable pubs.
Trouble finally erupted in Park Street and Great George Street when a large number of black troops gathered there that Saturday night. White troops objected and brawling broke out. Over four hundred black and white Americans were involved and it took 120 military police – known as Snowdrops because of their white helmets – to break it up.
The black troops were marched off down Park Street to the Centre where trucks were waiting to take them back to camp. On the way down, panic broke out as the Snowdrops used their clubs, and a black soldier who stabbed an MP with his knife was shot in the legs. Buses were drawn across the side roads to confine the incident and several men were seriously wounded. One died, and Bristol remained under military curfew for some days. While all this was going on, horrified Bristolians looked on, and some encouraged the black troops to resist. One 28 year-old woman was fined for assaulting a military policeman who was hitting a black G.I.
Other towns had problems, too. Citizens of Cheltenham, where American supply services were based, were polled on the race situation and concluded overwhelmingly that the treatment of the black soldiers by the whites was unsatisfactory; the white officers responded by calling the locals 'nigger-lovers'. In Westonbirt, where 1,000 black troops were encamped, a racist local farmer told his MP that he had to sit up all night with a shotgun because the black troops were causing terror and alarm. This was investigated and found to be

pure invention.

Taunton was out of bounds to black troops who had to go to Chard cinemas where there were separate seats for them. Yeovil had whole cinemas set aside for blacks, and certain pubs were off-limits to them. Being famous didn't help: when Joe Louis, the world-beating black boxer, went to a cinema at Salisbury, he was told to go and sit in the black section. The manager knew who he was and apologised, saying that he had instructions from the Army.

Bob Chapple recalls the problems caused by the race issue.

❝I was entertainments officer for the black G.I's and I learned a lot about the prejudice they suffered. To me they were good boys, they kept pretty much to themselves and loved their music. Living with them and working with them I came to understand their problems. The blacks rarely started trouble, they used to take a lot of flack before they responded. They were given strict instructions on how they were to behave; they were not supposed to carry knives, which they liked to do. The American Army was a law unto itself, it had its own rules and regulations and was policed by their own people. I remember one young black guy called Philips, he was 18, and he was down in Baldwin Street when there had been some trouble on the Centre, so he started running. Someone caught up with him and told him to stop, and when he didn't, they fired on him and he fell down dead.❞

One of the most notorious cases in the region was the Leroy Henry rape case at Bath. On the night of May 5, 1944, a 35-year-old English woman answered a knock on the door at her house in Combe Down and then claimed that the black GI outside pulled a knife and threatened to kill her if she didn't have sex with him. Bath police were called, Leroy was handed over to the military authorities and at a court-martial was found guilty of rape and sentenced to be hanged. His defence was that he had known the woman before, and had had sex with her for money, and that she made up the rape charge because she did not want her husband to know.

The Leroy case caused strong feelings, since rape was not a capital crime in Britain. A public petition was started, the *Daily Mirror* ran a campaign and eventually Eisenhower overturned the verdict and Leroy went back to normal duties. The experience of American racism at work in the West Country had left a nasty taste behind.

But in Europe, thanks to the Americans, the Allies were at last making progress and for most people this signalled the end of the war. Tragically, however, many women lost boyfriends and husbands in that last final push, among them Connie Whale.

❝We had a very hurried Utility wedding because my husband had been called abroad and we decided to get married before he went. We got a special licence and married without telling anyone. We had no witnesses, we had to find two strangers in the street. We had no reception, no honeymoon. I would have liked a posh wedding but it didn't worry me. And then my husband left. He was away long enough for my baby to be 15 months old, without having seen his father.

Then one evening I got a telegram and it had priority written on it so I knew what it was. It said his plane had failed to return from a raid over Frankfurt. I just started crying and I couldn't stop but at the back of my mind I kept thinking perhaps he's a prisoner, perhaps he'll come back. I went on waiting and hoping for months, every day I wrote in my diary 'no news', and then I had

The front page of the Evening Post, May 8, 1945.

notification that his plane had been found in the forest and that all the crew had perished.

Everyone said I was very brave but inside I was feeling terrible, and so sad for my little boy who would never know his Daddy. It took ages and ages to get back to normal again though I knew I had to for the sake of my baby. I felt so

angry against the Germans, thoughts kept going round my head, why did it have to happen, why did it have to be me, but my husband volunteered for the aircrew and I didn't want to stop him because he felt it was his duty. I've still got that telegram, it's falling to pieces.**'**

The VE Day crowd in the High Street and Corn Street hear a speech made from the Old Council House.

When victory finally arrived, Connie did not join in the wild rejoicing on VE Day.

'I felt a bit bitter. Everyone was celebrating but I felt I couldn't, I thought what have I got to celebrate, I've lost my husband, we were very much in love. I've still got John's photo on the sideboard, and sometimes I re-read my diaries and go through it all again, which is silly because it starts me off feeling sad. But I can't help doing it, I just want to re-live it and not forget.**'**

VE Day in the West Country, as all over Britain, was an uninhibited outpouring of all kinds of feelings, relief, joy, satisfaction, and underneath a sense of regret and bitterness at what the war had cost. But for one day, people went wild.

Bill Graves remembers:

'I happened to be at home for VE Day and well it was crazy, Bristol went crazy, we were dancing in the streets, doing the Conga all round the streets, and somehow landlords found some beer and a fair drop of booze was consumed. There were still some black Americans in the city and they all joined in.**'**

Doreen Owen was another who joined in the fun.

There'll Always Be An England: The VE Day celebrations in Bristol.

❝There was a little church hall not far from where we lived and there we had loads of parties and dancing and singing and things for children – we just went mad, we dressed up in fancy dress and decorated the street with flags. People dragged pianos out into the streets and the old lady next door came out and danced in her pinny.❞

Street parties were hastily organised and long hoarded food was brought out in amazing quantities, luxuries which had not been seen throughout the whole war, and there were unheard of treats like crackers and fireworks . . .
Gerald Smith:

❝This man had kept a box of fireworks all through the war and he started letting them off, and my brother was terrified, he ran around saying don't, don't, you shouldn't do this, because they were a reminder of war, not peace . . . it was a wonderful day, the church bells rang for hours, and that was out of this world because we hadn't heard them for years. We had bonfires in the streets and food I hadn't seen before came out. And the American soldiers came with their lorries and packed people in tight, and they took us all round the city to see what was going on. It was mayhem for two days, sheer joy. Nobody went to bed.❞

There were similar scenes everywhere; at Avonmouth ships' flags decorated the streets and the pubs were drunk dry. In Taunton, hundreds congregated for an open-air, non-stop church service which went on into the small hours until the clergy's voices were hoarse.
And then the Americans went home – leaving behind broken hearts, and a

new social problem.

In Bristol, the *Sunday Pictorial* recorded, there were scenes of anguish in August 1945 as hundreds of screaming girls aged 17-25 besieged the barracks where the black soldiers were packing up. They broke down barriers and sang 'Don't Fence Me In', and the gates of the railway station were rushed by girls who allegedly said: "To hell with the US colour bar, we want our coloured sweethearts."

Journalistic licence perhaps, but the black soldiers had certainly won more than hearts as the 'brown babies' scandal afterwards proved. These were the half-caste children born to the black GI's British girlfriends; most of them ended up in orphanages because at the time it was thought too much of a social stigma for their mothers to keep them. The numbers of white babies with GI fathers was never calculated, but in Gloucestershire U.S. Army leaflets were handed out telling mothers how to trace their boyfriends and claim paternity allowance.

Somerset County Council set up a nursery near Minehead for 37 of these brown babies, who were taken from their mothers at two weeks old. The need for haste was obvious: 27 of the babies were born to married women and their husbands were due to be demobbed. None of the mothers made any inquiry about the subsequent fate of their children, whom the authorities believed would never be adopted because of their colour.

A BBC reporter gets a reaction to the news of peace, from a Bristol bus queue in the Centre, May 1945.

Gloucestershire had the same problem on their hands with 60 'brown babies', Devon had 83, and Cornwall 38. In Bristol the story that Southmead Hospital had been turned into a maternity unit for girls having black babies was so persistent that it had to be officially denied in the press by the city's Medical Officer of Health.

This was the one of the few times the presence of the Americans in the West was officially admitted, for security as ever was tight, even though everyone, down to the smallest child who rejoiced in the Americans' amazing Christmas parties knew that they were here, and why. It was back to austerity when they left. Now the people had to win the peace, in a completely different world.

For the war had changed people irrevocably: they vowed they were never going back to the misery of the Thirties. War had broadened their experience, opened their eyes to social conditions, and made them suspicious of the class who ran the country. A mood of idealism was abroad, remembers Joyce Storey.

‘We dreamed of a better tomorrow, a socialist Britain, it was our Utopia. It would give the working class a bigger slice of the cake and there would be equal opportunities for all.’

Bill Graves, later to become a Labour Councillor, shared her views.

‘I grew up in an area of deprivation, though I wasn't deprived myself, and after the war people said ‘we're not going back to that life, we've stuck the war out and now we're going to have something better.'’

It was this feeling that won Labour the 1945 election: it was not so much a vote on the conduct of the war as a verdict on the ten years which preceded it. Joyce Storey remembers the euphoria in Bristol after the Labour victory.

‘It was like VE Day all over again, people were dancing in the streets and hugging one another. We thought this was it, all we'd dreamed about, the welfare state, free medicine, better housing was all round the corner.’

Bill Graves:

‘It was going to be the New Britain, we were going to be responsible for our own communities, we were going to have community councils, we would plan our city and set up a task force to build new houses – and it never came to pass.’

In fact grim austerity in Britain lasted into the Fifties, like the rationing and the scarred bomb sites blooming with buddleia and campion. Bristol's recovery from the war, as elsewhere, was slow and painful.

Fifty years on, the people who lived through the time when the West was at war have been taking stock of those terrible, comradely, exciting, dreary years, and revealing what the war made of them. They have calculated what the aftermath of that war was, and how their hearts and minds and habits were changed by those formative experiences.

Ask any member of the war generation and he or she will say this: it changed me, and changed my life. On a simple level, the war generated lifetime habits: an attachment to listening to news bulletins, of eating too much bread, of drinking too much tea. The war generation is thrifty and hates waste. They switch off lights, and never waste food, or throw away clothes. They still make-

do and mend.

Barbara Stinchcombe, a child during the war, says:

‘ The war made me value people, not things. My husband and I both escaped death – I was due to be evacuated to Canada on ‘The City of Benares’ which was sunk, and my husband and his mother ran for and missed one of the Broadmead buses that was burned. So we both feel our lives are a gift to us. The war taught me to be prepared for disappointments. All through it, I begged my mother for a doll’s pram, but there wasn’t one to be had, and in a strange way I think this early disappointment taught me to bear the fact that I was never able to have a real baby to push in a real pram. I think the war generation are happier with simple pleasures. It’s not the end of the world if you don’t get what you want. ’

But there were adverse effects too, which came from missed educational chances, separation and childhood bereavements, and shattered nerves. Even now, some of the war generation still flinch at the sound of a siren, or a loud plane flying overhead. Moreen Sellars has suffered from depression all her life, something her psychiatrist traces back to her terrifying war experiences.

‘ I do not look back upon wartime with any affection. It has affected me for life. My feeling is that life is short and terribly precious and that everyone should treasure what they have. I always want people to be happy and safe and I get into terrible depressions if there is a death, or a rift in the family. I’m sure this is linked with my experiences in the blitz when I had to be responsible for my family. I cope well in a crisis but I collapse afterwards. I’m full of insecurity

The Americans were famous for their fantastic Christmas parties for children. An American Santa and his team are presenting a marionette show.

The day the hoarded food came out at last: a street party celebration on VE Day. This one took place in Brislington.

and it was the war that caused it. **9**

Others, like Amy Granton, take a more positive view.

6 I always feel very fortunate. We were in the thick of it and we came through and it made me learn the value of everything. I feel I am a better person for going through it. **9**

Babs Atherton:

6 The war made me personally more independent. My husband was in the army for five years, I had a daughter in 1944 and I was on my own, I had to cope. I learned a lot from having to do without things, and that taught me to manage better when supplies got more plentiful later on. **9**

Everyone mourned the lost landscapes of their cities and towns, for so much had vanished for ever. Gerald Smith:

6 You couldn't take it in, there was the cinema you used to go to, the church you used to go to, your library, gone up in flames. Park Street was a row of twisted girders, Castle Street where we shopped was gone, and even now you still remember the old city that disappeared, and feel a certain guilt that you survived when so much and so many didn't. **9**

Gladys Locke, whose story opened this book:

‘Every night I used to make a bargain with God: 'Please God, spare me and I will never be miserable again.' It was a wicked thing to do but that's what I actually did. War made you think what a wonderful thing life is, so you used to promise God you'd be an ideal person if you were spared. Of course after the war, you almost forgot it all, how everyone had been friendly, fighting in a common cause. I learned, too, that not all Germans were monsters. After the war we had a pre-fab and we had some German prisoners of war to do our garden. They were the two nicest boys I have ever met. They were so kind, they made toys for my children. It was amazing, I used to think 'these same boys were up there bombing us, and we were bombing them' and yet I was really fond of those two German boys.’

For some of the interviewees in this book, their stories are a memorial to the family and friends who died, a litany for the dead, whose names they will never forget.

For the final reckoning in the West Country was a terrible one. In Bristol, 1,299 died, 3,305 were injured, 3,000 homes destroyed, and 90,000 damaged. In Somerset, 668 died, 1,608 were injured, and 35,000 homes damaged or destroyed. In Bath, 417 died, 873 were injured, 19,147 homes were hit; in Weston-super-Mare, 102 died, 338 were injured and 8,574 homes damaged or destroyed. In Gloucestershire, 237 died, 696 were injured and 2,400 properties hit.

Every one of those statistics hides a human tragedy.

Arthur Backhurst, who as a young man survived the raid on BAC at Filton, never forgets his workmates who died.

‘I always think about them, even now. I have a photograph of the bronze memorial plaque that's in the Filton canteen, and I get it out every now and then and go through all the names, and think about them. There was Mervyn Prewitt and Jimmy Ratchford, George Hill, Arthur Plunkett and Vyvian Roberts . . . and I feel sad. It was all a long time ago, but yes, you feel sad.’

Some of the most striking images of World War II in these pages were the work of the outstanding Bristol photo-journalist Jim Facey.

Jim joined the staff of the *Evening Post*'s predecessor, the *Bristol Times & Echo* as a boy. After the paper was closed down, Jim was one of the chosen few invited to set up the *Evening Post* in 1932.

His courageous coverage of the unemployment riots in Old Market – he was attacked by demonstrators and took the classic picture of the police baton charge by breaking an upstairs window and photographing through the broken pane of glass – earned him the World Press Medal as photographer of the year. The award was presented to him by the great British journalist Hannen Swaffer.

When World War II broke out, Jim was the *Post*'s picture editor and chief photographer. He showed skill, flair and considerable bravery, often leaving the relative safety of air raid shelters to photograph the raids as they happened. He realised that many of his war-time pictures would never be published at the time. They were too strong, too emotive to pass the censor's scrutiny, but that did not deter him. He took the pictures anyway.

He was so well-known on Bristol's war-time scene that when Queen Mary, the then Queen Mother, spotted him and he failed to notice her, she gave him a cheerful prod in the back with her umbrella. 'Come on Jim,' she called out, 'get on with your work.'

The pictures have a rare quality. Besides documenting the damage and the nightmare quality of a city under fire, they also emphasise the plight of ordinary people caught up in a great conflict, the women and children who suffered as well as the volunteers who did so much to help the victims. The little girl whose doll's house survived the destruction of Newfoundland Road in central Bristol, and the warden working into the unstable ruins of a house in St Michael's Hill where two women lie buried are just two examples of his narrative style.

That Jim Facey took a great pride in his war pictures is shown in the fact that of all the countless thousands of images he took in a lifetime's career as a photographer, the one album of original prints he kept at home was of war pictures, more than 100 of them. This unique record, which contains some images never published before, has been carefully preserved by his son Dave, to whom the authors, Domino Films and HTV West express their gratitude for permission to reproduce these pictures.

After the war, Jim left journalism and set up the successful commercial photography firm of Tudor, Facey and Miller from which he retired at the age of 65. He died in 1977.

Despite the success of the company – there must be hundreds of Bristol couples whose wedding was captured on film by the familiar figure of Jim Facey – Jim remained a journalist at heart, his former colleagues say.

One, George Gallop, said: 'He was totally committed to his work and he

Jim Facey, jaunty as ever, among the troops, camera to hand, cigarette in mouth. Jim was such a well-known character on Bristol's war-time scene that Queen Mary, then the Queen Mother, prodded him with her umbrella when he failed to notice her on one occasion.

never really ceased to be a photo-journalist . . . and a great one at that. "Impact and punch", that was the catchphrase he used when he was teaching me. He went to the heart of his subjects – his war pictures show that clearly.'